BULLETPROOF RETIREMENT

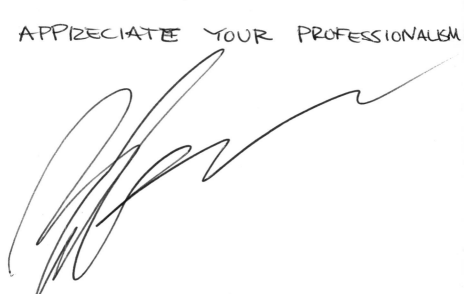

Bob—

It was an honor to be on your show. I appreciate your professionalism

The ideas and opinions in this publication are solely those of its author. The author and the publisher are not engaged in rendering financial, investment legal or other professional advice. If such advice, services or assistance is required, the counsel of a competent professional should be pursued. Both the author and publisher specifically disclaim any responsibility for any liability, loss or risk, personal or otherwise, which is incurred as a consequence, directly or indirectly of the use and application of any of the contents of this book.

For my wife, Sheryl,
a partner in life whose belief in me
has made this book possible.

ACKNOWLEDGMENTS

Although this was the second book I have written, it was not any easier and I would like to thank the people who helped make it a reality. I would like to thank Alan Horowitz and Larry Weist for their editing comments. Special thanks to Kirk Bennett, Greg Damron, Kelly Dangerfield, Chris Light and Brett Munson for reading the book numerous times to make sure the content was correct and for the time they spent doing research for the book. I would like to thank Nicki Fuller for the time she spent making all the changes to the text. Also, I would like to thank my entire staff for the countless times they all read the book to ensure that it made sense.

Without the help of these people, this book would not have been possible.

CONTENTS

BULLETPROOFING WORKS

In 1991, I wrote, *Bulletproof Your Financial Future,* a book that provided people at all stages of life with advice on how to create the most effective investment strategies for their needs at that moment. I am now writing this book specifically for those who are retired, near retirement or planning their retirement.

In the years since my first book, I have learned a lot about the financial world from investing to estate planning, and these insights of course, have been included throughout this book. However, the primary reason for writing this book is that Bulletproofing, which I will describe shortly, is so well suited for retirement. Bulletproofing provides you with protection against the ebbs and flows of the economy over time. While there are no guarantees in life—or in personal finance— Bulletproofing will help secure your financial retirement.

The proof, they say, is in the pudding. Look at Figure 1 and you will see that in a seven-year period that included the three down years after the tech bubble burst, two flat years and two good years, we still managed to have average returns of more than 10 percent a year during that period. This provided investors with almost a double on their investments in the medium-risk portfolio devised by Lefavi Wealth Management. Disclosures for this and the rest of the figures in this book can be found in Appendix F.

I chose this portfolio because it is the one used by the majority of my clients and is the portfolio where I keep my

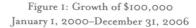

Figure I: Growth of $100,000
January I, 2000–December 31, 2006

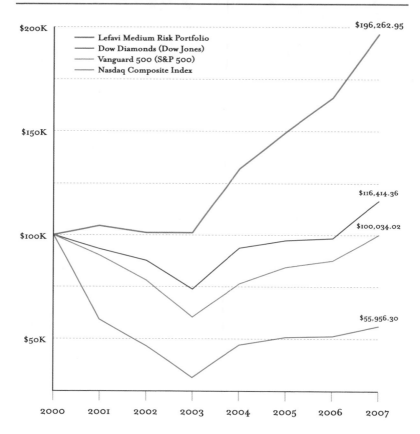

personal investments. The objective of the medium-risk portfolio is to earn 12 percent and I always tell my clients we aim for
12 percent, but if we get 10 percent, be happy. To get 10 percent during the seven years that included the worst downturn
in the markets since the Great Depression and surviving that
without a loss is absolutely stunning by anyone's analysis. What
makes it even more amazing is that it was done with roughly
one-half to two-thirds of overall market risk.

The medium-risk portfolio gives my clients enough risk exposure to produce good investment returns, but not so much that they are uncomfortable. Of course, some clients prefer less risk and others more, and I have portfolios to meet their needs, but the medium-risk portfolio is my most popular portfolio.

I think you should analyze any portfolio's performance by what it does in the bad times. This is the real key to having a successful portfolio. If you drop in half during the down times, your investments have to double to get you back where you started. In my mind, this is an unacceptable position to be in and that is why we Bulletproof.

In addition, I chose this seven-year period because it was the beginning of a new millennium and was when I first started using the recommendations I make on my radio show in my clients' portfolios. Using these recommendations takes advantage of my "devastation dividends approach," which is outlined later in this chapter. Also, there is the rule of 72, which is, when you divide the rate of return into 72, that tells you the length of time it takes to double your investments. With a return of 10 percent, it takes 7.2 years and we had almost a double with an average annual return of 10.11 percent from January 1, 2000 through January 1, 2007.

My Strategy Works

The Dow Diamonds is an exchange-traded fund that tracks the Dow Jones Industrial Average. If you want a portion of your portfolio to follow the Dow, you would buy a fund like the Dow Diamonds (otherwise, you would have to buy all 30 stocks that make up the Dow). The Vanguard 500 Index is probably the best-known fund that mirrors the performance of the S&P 500. If you want to have a portion of your portfolio follow the S&P 500, you would buy a fund like the Vanguard 500 (otherwise, you would have to buy all 500 stocks that make up the S&P 500). If you wanted your portfolio to follow the NASDAQ, you would use the NASDAQ composite index, which is made up of all the stocks in the NASDAQ.

Let's see how the performance of the Lefavi Medium-Risk Portfolio compared with the Dow Diamonds, the Vanguard 500 and the NASDAQ composite index. From January 1, 2000 through January 1, 2007, the Dow Diamonds had an annual rate of return of 2.20 percent, and for the period, a cumulative return of 16.41 percent. The Vanguard 500 had an annual rate of return of 0.01 percent, and a cumulative gain of 0.03 percent. The NASDAQ composite index got hammered the worst and was down 44.4 percent for those seven years. The Lefavi Medium-Risk Portfolio had an average annual rate of return of 10.11 percent, as mentioned before, and a cumulative return of 96.26 percent.

For retirees, my performance is even more impressive than these figures suggest. During the seven years from the beginning of 2000 through the end of 2006, the medium-risk portfolio didn't take a loss in the three years from the beginning of 2000 through the end of 2002 and had substantial gains in the four years from the beginning 2003 through the end of 2006. Consistency like this is valuable; it lets you sleep well at night.

The Dow Diamonds had losses in three of the seven years, as did the Vanguard 500. In fact, in no year did the Dow Diamonds or Vanguard 500 outperform the Lefavi Medium-Risk Portfolio.

I was just reading that the typical 65-year-old-man today could expect to live to 81, while the 65-year-old-woman can expect to live to 85. More than 17 percent of today's 65-year-old men and 31 percent of today's 65-year-old women are expected to live to age 90 or beyond. (Department of Retirement Systems, State of Washington) If you are a couple where both of you are 65 years old and you want to make sure your money lasts as long as both of you, there's a better than

30 percent chance that at least one of you will live past 90, which means your money has to last another 25-plus years. To be on the safe side, you would probably plan for it to last 30 years or more.

That is why it is imperative that you have some growth in your investments or your purchasing power will be eroded over time. Studies show that if you had all of your money in fixed incomes such as CDs, between taxes and inflation, it would erode your purchasing power by 1.45 percent per year. See Appendix A, which will show you the decline of value of a certificate of deposit. Figure 2 shows a very conservative U.S. stock fund, Investment Company of America, compared to using CDs (assuming the investor earns the average rate of return for a 6-month CD each year). It shows that if you start out with $500,000 and withdraw $35,000 a year, you would run out of money after about 15 years if you were to use a CD. However, the value of the stock fund increases during the entire period. This is why having some growth is a necessity if you are to keep pace with inflation and have enough money to spend in your later years.

Also, take a look at Figure 3 which shows you different types of investments you could have such as CDs, the Dow Jones Industrial Average, the Vanguard 500 index and the Lefavi Medium-Risk Portfolio. As you can see, if you are not able to diversify enough to Bulletproof, it can be devastating to your returns. You must also have some growth, which is why CDs are, again, a bad choice. Also, non-diversified portfolios are big losers when compared to our Bulletproofing approach. No matter how you look at it, if you are a medium-risk investor, my medium-risk portfolio is the way to go. Bulletproofing works. Period.

The Really Stupid: Buying Certificates of Depreciation (or what other people call Certificates of Deposit).

Figure 2: $500,000 Investment Withdrawing $35,000
Per Year Using Real Returns

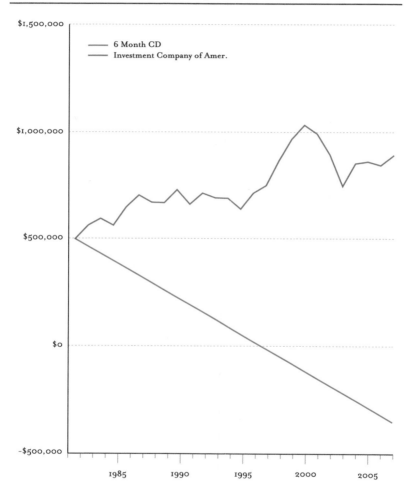

No one can predict what will happen 10 years from now, let alone 30. This is why protecting your investment dollars is essential. That is what Bulletproofing does. It protects your investment dollars so you will have enough money to last you and your spouse to the end of your retirements.

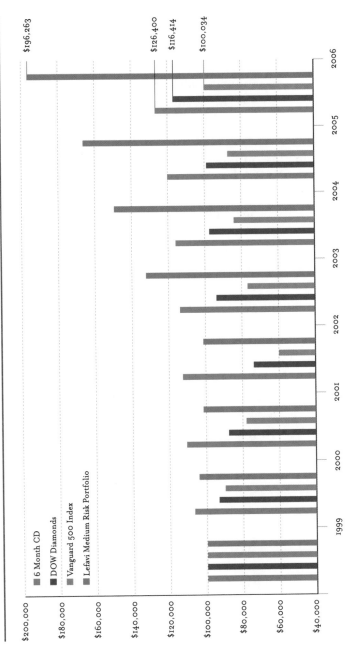

Figure 3: Comparison of Different Investments

BRUCE'S LAWS

These are the laws my firm is run by:

1. Don't lose money. Bulletproofing your portfolio is the answer to this. It provides the keys to protecting yourself by investing for the long term with good, solid investments. See explanation on Bulletproofing for the details.

2. Don't lose money then make a buck. You can't make any money if you lose money. Most of the people I see lost about half of what they had when the tech bubble burst because of their poor investment strategy. To repeat myself, if you drop in half, you have to have a double to get back to even. That's a steep hill to climb. Not losing money is the key to all financial success.

3. No surprises. I run my firm this way because I believe my clients should be kept informed through my radio show, monthly letters, quarterly financial reports, annual in-person reviews, and my Client Appreciation Day. Our objective is to make full disclosure of everything from fees to costs to ensure clients are informed of what they are getting. *Any financial adviser you work with should be willing to do the same.*

4. Do everything in our power to protect our client's financial interests. We try to cover every aspect of our client's financial well being from insurance to estate planning, to make sure the money is always there for them.

5. Whatever the government gets involved in, they make worse. Their heavy-handed approach to everything and their incredibly non-responsive and stupid bureaucracies simply make it difficult to succeed any time there is heavy government involvement. If you ever see a situation where they are passing more laws to regulate a certain industry, that is probably an industry you are not going to want to invest in.

THREE STEPS TO A BULLETPROOF PORTFOLIO

1. Bulletproofing
2. Modern Portfolio Theory
3. Devastation Dividends

BULLETPROOFING

Since Bulletproofing protects one's assets no matter what the economy does, it is particularly suited for retirement planning. When your investment portfolio is Bulletproofed, you can rest easy because the ups-and-downs the economy invariably takes will not have long-lasting effects on your financial future.

Bulletproofing isn't magic. It takes a small portion of your investments and puts them into assets that typically go up when the economy goes down in a recession or depression (in particular, long-term U.S. government bonds), or that go up sharply when inflation is roaring along (hard assets as real estate and gold).

Think of Bulletproofing as a form of insurance. Let me give you an analogy: your home. Your home is probably worth hundreds of thousands, even millions of dollars. You protect it from intruders by having locks on your windows and doors, maybe an alarm system, and perhaps outdoor lighting that turns on when it senses movement. For fire, you have smoke alarms and a fire extinguisher, and possibly a sprinkler system. In the event of power problems, you protect your electronic gizmos with surge protectors, battery backups and perhaps a power generator. In addition, you buy insurance to protect against financial losses from burglary, fire, and other potential harmful occurrences.

When you consider the costs of all this protection, it is small, even trivial, compared with the value of the assets you are protecting. Bulletproofing works in a similar fashion. At very little cost or even a profit, which virtually all of these investments make over the long term, it protects what is probably your largest and most important financial asset—your retirement funds. And, it does so by placing small portions cf your portfolio into assets that are likely to go up when the economy is faltering. With these assets in place, what the economy does becomes of much less importance to you.

Let's say inflation gets up a head of steam and becomes higher than you ever thought possible (remember that as recently as the late 1970s and early 1980s, inflation was running at an annual 10 percent-plus rate). When Bulletproofing is done correctly, your assets should rise sufficiently in value to cover the increased costs you will incur because of the higher inflation.

Bulletproofing is, however, a broader concept than just investing. It is about protecting yourself from anything that can harm you financially. From having the proper insurance so that people cannot sue you and take your investments away to helping you reduce taxes so you avoid unnecessary expenses, including payment to Uncle Sam. Protecting yourself also involves asset protection including what types of entities you should use to divide and protect your assets such as a C or S corporation, a limited liability company, a family limited partnership, an offshore or Nevada trust. Basically, what you really need and how you should use it.

Estate planning cannot be ignored as one of the areas that Bulletproofing addresses. This is important to help ensure your assets go to who you want them to instead of the taxman and the attorneys. Identity theft and what you need to do in order to protect yourself in today's complex world. We are constantly updating these areas and if you would like to get the latest information, call and get a free copy of Bruce's Best Information on these topics.

I recommend that you work with a financial advisor who addresses all of these areas. Even if you don't use my firm, use someone who is willing to tackle these complex issues to ensure that you are protected in every aspect of your life. In addition, we do extensive reporting to our clients to keep them informed through-out the year. We do this through my weekly radio show, which can be heard 24 hours a day on my website www.lefavi.com. We also send our easy-to-understand quarterly financial statements to all clients and monthly letters addressing issues I think are vitally im-portant to everyone's financial well being.

On a more personal level, I do annual reviews with all of my clients to go over any questions and apprise clients of in-formation that affects them. An example of this is when the HIPAA law was passed it changed the ability for people to have their affairs handled properly. If you were injured or disabled, your family couldn't get your medical information without a HIPAA form. Without your medical information, they cannot be appointed to handle your financial affairs. We solved this problem by having our attorneys creating a HIPAA form that we gave to each client at their annual review. In addition, we helped each client fill the form out and we notarized them so they were able to avoid a problem most of them didn't even know existed.

Our big event every year is Client Appreciation Day where we bring in experts from all over the country to keep our clients informed on various issues. We have had speakers such as governors, Federal Reserve Board members, doctors and disciplinarians of every kind. This provides a way for our clients to stay informed and learn about a variety of subjects.

MODERN PORTFOLIO THEORY

As a money manager and investment advisor, I place most of my client's assets according to a sophisticated investment strategy I modeled on what is called "Modern Portfolio The-ory." This theory minimizes the risks of investing while maxi-mizing returns by diversifying one's portfolio. Diversification is simply putting your money into a broad range of different assets, rather than relying on one or a few types of assets. It has been proven that proper diversification based on Modern Portfolio Theory can sometimes even boost returns while lowering risks. I didn't create Modern Portfolio Theory. The three economists who did, won the Nobel Prize in Economics for their work. When some economic genius creates a theory and proves it, and then wins a Nobel Prize, I pay attention. We will discuss Modern Portfolio Theory more in Chapter 6.

DEVASTATION DIVIDENDS

I am always looking at what is happening in the domestic and world economy, the stock market, various industries, government tax and other policies, and all the other factors that can affect the performance of my clients' portfolios. When I see anomalies—something unusual going on that suggests a certain investment is likely to do well or poorly—I mention this to the listeners of my radio show and talk about it with my clients.

These insights help boost the performance of my clients' portfolios above and beyond just what my Bulletproofing and Modern Portfolio Theory would produce. I call these devastation dividends because the investments I recommend to my clients usually involve a situation where something has happened, the market has over responded (or not yet responded) and there is now an opportunity for savvy investors to buy on the cheap and boost their returns; you get a dividend based on the devastation some asset has experienced.

Below are the predictions I made on my radio program that pointed to devastation dividends listeners could incorporate into their own investments. I list them so you can see that my claim of being able to spot opportunities is not just a meaningless boast. These were predictions I made in public, on the radio, where tens of thousands of people heard them and I have tape recordings to prove I made them.

In case you are wondering why my predictions are so accurate, I'll tell you my "secret"—common sense. That's what I use. In truth, not that many people in the investment advisory business have much common sense. In addition to common sense, I invest for the long-term, which reduces the risk. This is why my predictions are usually right; if you invest in good things and hold for the long-term, you are almost always right. That is a key secret to being successful financially.

Note: These predictions are not to be considered specific investment advice or recommendations, but useful insights, observations, and consumer tips that may help people benefit from major market moves and trends. We have included only the predictions that were completed by the end of 2006, meaning they were either deemed successful or unsuccessful. This is consistent with the seven-year period we have been discussing beginning January 1, 2000 to January 1, 2007.

1997 PREDICTIONS

1. On Saturday, January 11, 1997, I broadcast a show on "The Danger of Hedge Funds." I said that, eventually, some hedge funds would fail and that these funds were extremely dangerous. I suggested that investors consider staying away from hedge funds.

   Later that year, Long-Term Capital Management's hedge fund ran into serious financial trouble and, in September 1998, had to be bailed out to the tune of $3.5 billion by the Federal Reserve Bank. The reason the Federal Reserve decided to bail out the hedge fund was because it was afraid of a shock to the entire system of world markets in the event of

potential failure of this single hedge fund. This one
example shows the incredible stupidity and risk involved in many hedge funds and the reason I predicted,
correctly, there would be serious problems with them.
SUCCESSFUL

2. In October of 1997, I said, "Don't buy cars. The prices
are going to fall."

I was exactly right. The prices on automobiles fell
thereafter and, by the end of the year, most carmakers
had introduced incentives with discounts as high as
$3,000. SUCCESSFUL

3. At the beginning of the year, in the same show where I
predicted that hedge funds would have problems, I predicted that prices of used cars would fall.

Used car prices fell in April by 4.1 percent. In May,
they were down 3.7 percent. In June, they were down
2.4 percent. People who took my advice and held off
buying a new or used car during 1997 saved a lot of
money. SUCCESSFUL

1998 PREDICTIONS

4. During the Pacific Rim crisis, I predicted two things:

First, I predicted that the crisis would spread.

The crisis did spread to South America and across the
Pacific Rim to virtually all the Third-World nations.
SUCCESSFUL

5. Second, I said that, as investors searched for security,
Treasury Bonds would rise in value.

Treasury Bonds continued to have solid returns for the
five years following my prediction. The Lehman Broth-

ers Long Treasury Bond Index had a cumulative return of 57.98 percent from June 1998 through May 2003. SUCCESSFUL

6. In 1998, the Roth IRA became available. At that time, I predicted that many of the loopholes in the Roth IRA would be corrected, making the investment less financially beneficial. I predicted that the Roth IRA laws would be changed soon and changed often. I warned investors to be very careful when taking advantage of the obvious loopholes.

   This sequence occurred as predicted. In 1998, after the law had been in effect only six months, the Roth IRA laws were overhauled completely, trapping many investors. SUCCESSFUL

1999 PREDICTIONS

7. In 1999, I predicted that actively managed funds would dramatically outperform index funds. I believed the rapid growth of online trading would create a herd effect where people would stampede in and out of various securities, increasing volatility. This would create a situation where the actively managed funds would outperform the indexes because managers could see what was happening in a given situation and move their investments around accordingly. On the other hand, index investors would be subject to the whims of the herd.

   As predicted, a majority of the actively managed funds outperformed their relative index, and some of the best funds outperformed the indexes by more than 20 percent that year. SUCCESSFUL

8. In June 1999, I predicted value funds would outperform income-oriented stock funds. The reason was that the Federal Reserve raised interest rates and was most likely going to continue to do so in the near future. This indicated that income-oriented stock funds would not do well during this period. In fact, the investments that should do well are the value funds because of the pressure placed on the income-oriented funds for the conservative investor.

   As it turned out, value funds in general outperformed equity income funds for the year. Morningstar's Large-Cap Value Index was up 18.43 percent from January 2, 2001 to December 31, 2004, a period when the Dow was up only 1.28 percent. SUCCESSFUL

9. I also predicted in June 1999 that, because the Federal Reserve was embarking on a path of increasing interest rates, sooner or later the stock market would be forced down.

   This, of course, happened in 1999, but was followed by a boom when it looked like the Federal Reserve wasn't going to increase interest rates any more. This was followed by another bust in 2000 as the Fed continued to raise interest rates. SUCCESSFUL

10. In 1999, I said some investors would be absolutely destroyed by a sudden drop in the NASDAQ market.

    This happened in May 2000 when the NASDAQ was down 38 percent, causing some leveraged investors to lose everything. SUCCESSFUL

11. In June 1999, I predicted that once the Federal Reserve raised interest rates, it would continue to raise interest rates for at least a year. A known characteristic of the Federal Reserve is that, once it embarks on a path, it stays on that path. It does not raise interest rates one month

and lower them the following month. It continues to raise or lower interest rates until it gets the turnaround in the economy it is looking for.

The Federal Reserve raised interest rates .25 percent in June 1999 and continued to raise them until mid-year 2000. SUCCESSFUL

2000 PREDICTIONS

12. In January 2000, I predicted a large drop in technology stocks.

   Said drop occurred in May with a 38 percent decrease in the NASDAQ. Friday, May 26, 2000, the NASDAQ reached a relative low of 3,205.11. SUCCESSFUL

13. In April, I predicted the financial and biotechnology sectors would be good places to invest. On May 27, 2000, I predicted that it was the time to start buying large-cap tech stocks.

   The Dow Jones Financial Index was up nearly 25 percent from April 1 through December 31, 2000, and the AMEX Biotechnology Index was up nearly 27 percent over the same period. Also, as predicted, large-cap technologies jumped drastically over the short-term. From May 27 through September 1, 2000, the NASDAQ 100 jumped more than 32 percent. SUCCESSFUL

14. In March, I predicted that REITs would be a good investment.

   REITs hit a bottom around that time then went straight up, some jumping up over 20 percent in less than one month. SUCCESSFUL

2001 PREDICTIONS

15. In January 2001, I foresaw falling interest rates and, as
     the market was quite risky, predicted that conservative
     income-oriented investments such as income funds and
     all types of bonds would do well.

     In 2001, the discount rate fell drastically—it went from
     6 percent in December 2000 down to 1.25 percent in Janu-
     ary 2002. During 2001, the Lehman Brothers Aggregate
     Bond Index rose 8.44 percent and, according to Morning-
     star, funds with income as their objective were up 5.44 per-
     cent, each above their 5-year averages. SUCCESSFUL

16. In January 2001, I also predicted that value stocks and
     utilities would do well because they are generally more
     conservative than many growth-oriented investments.

     These asset classes were slower to react but are continu-
     ing to be solid investment areas. The Dow Jones Utility
     Index increased more than 68 percent from January
     2003 through December 2004, and Morningstar's U.S.
     Value Index was up 51.62 percent during that same pe-
     riod. SUCCESSFUL

17. Also in January, I again predicted that actively managed
     funds would outperform index funds because index
     funds were over-weighted in technology.

     The average index fund was down 9 percent for the year.
     About half of the actively managed funds outperformed
     the indexes, and the actively managed funds I liked dra-
     matically outperformed the indexes. SUCCESSFUL

18. In May 2001, I predicted Asian markets would be strong
     performers, Korea in particular. The reason was that
     Korea made the changes to its banking system necessary in
     order for it to succeed. In the past, loans were made in
     Korea, as in Japan, based on connections rather than

merit. Korea made the changes necessary to correct that problem where the Japanese didn't. In addition, many fine stocks in Korea were selling for pennies on the dollar. I thought it represented a unique opportunity at that time.

Since then, most Korean funds have performed exceptionally. The MSCI Korea Index was up more than 118 percent from May 2001 through December 2004. SUCCESSFUL

2002 PREDICTIONS

19. On September 22, 2002, I predicted that the market had reached a good buying level and said that buying stocks of any kind was a good idea.

In September 2003, the Dow was approaching 9,600, up nearly 1,600 points from the time, a year earlier, when I made my prediction. The Dow Jones Industrial Average exceeded 10,600 by year-end 2004. SUCCESSFUL

2003 PREDICTIONS

20. On March 8, 2003, I made an official prediction that it was a good time to buy high-yield (junk) bonds. At that time, they were at a significant low and I love investments that are down significantly.

High-yield bonds rose considerably during the rest of 2003. As an illustration, according to Morningstar, funds with a high-yield bond objective were up more then 20 percent from March 1, 2003 to December 31, 2003. SUCCESSFUL

21. On July 19, 2003, I predicted that Pacific Rim investments would do well. In particular, I believed that China
funds needed to be part of a person's portfolio because
of the tremendous potential in the way China was taking
to the free enterprise system. The 1.3 billion Chinese
represented a huge market and it was just starting to be
exploited at this time. The potential over the long term
was fantastic.

The MSCI Pacific Index was up 55.24 percent from July
2003 to December 2004, illustrating the growth the Pacific Rim was experiencing. SUCCESSFUL

2004 PREDICTIONS

22. On October 2, 2004, I predicted that master limited
partnerships would be one of the good investments at
the time. I felt strongly that real estate was overvalued
and that the average P/E ratio of the market was high.
The only thing in the market that seemed to represent a
real bargain was the more conservative master limited
partnerships.

On May 9, 2005, the MLPs that I recommended were
up an average of 13 percent and paid a 3 percent or
more dividend. During the same period, the Dow
dropped approximately 1.5 percent. This means the
MLPs outperformed the market by 17.5 percent,
total. SUCCESSFUL

23. In the third quarter of 2004, I predicted that real estate
was a very bad investment and, in fact, was experiencing
a bubble. I indicated that I had no idea when the bubble
might burst, but it was inevitable that sooner or later
there would be a downturn in the real estate market that

could prove to be quite severe. I recommended that investors stay away from real estate and, if they were considering purchasing, to purchase after a downturn in the market. SUCCESSFUL

2005 PREDICTIONS

24. On, March 12, 2005, I predicted that India funds would be a good investment. I believed that India had dramatically changed its business laws to favor industry. Most provinces offer huge tax incentives and, in some cases, businesses can operate virtually tax fee. I felt there was little doubt that India would go through a tremendous growth period. It is the second-most populous nation in the world with about 1 billion people and a sizable portion of the population being highly educated. This is a perfect breeding ground for rampant free enterprise. I believed that India funds would be a good, long-term, volatile investment.

   From March of 2005 to March of 2006, the India Fund that we used had a total return of 88 percent. SUCCESSFUL

2006 PREDICTIONS

25. On May 6, 2006, I stated that the 50 largest stocks are selling at the lowest P/E ratio compared to all the other groups of stocks in the S&P 500 index. This is the stock of companies that are big, strong, cash rich, dividend paying, and very secure. This usually means that because they are so secure they are going to sell at a higher P/E ratio than the other companies in the S&P 500 index.

I believe this is one of the few bargains that exist in the marketplace today. What generally happens is that the glamour of the small caps and the emerging markets attract money like a magnet, this makes other investments like the large-cap value stocks an incredible buy. If you buy stocks that are relatively low in price and hold for the long term, it is difficult to be wrong.

Over the period of May 1st, 2006 to April 30th, 2007 the Dow Jones Industrial Average (large-cap) was up 12.83% while the Russell 2000 Index (small-cap) was up only 4.19%. SUCCESSFUL

You now have an idea of my approach to investing, the kinds of investments I place my clients in and why my strategy is so well suited toward those planning for or in retirement. The remainder of the book will provide you with the specifics of how to use Bulletproofing to make your retirement as financially comfortable and secure as possible.

DEPRESSION BULLETPROOFING

A SHADOW FROM THE PAST

If you want to protect yourself financially if the economy gets into a deep, deep hole . . .

If you want to remove any concern you have about living through a difficult economy . . .

If you want to minimize your financial risk and Bulletproof your investment portfolio . . .

You need to read this chapter.

Rare is the person who goes through life without experiencing major turning points—moments that produce dramatic, permanent change.

Such moments may be psychological, but many are based on economic situations. No single economic event demonstrated this more powerfully than the Great Depression of the 1930s, a time few Americans survived emotionally or financially unscarred.

Until the day she died decades after the Depression, my friend's grandmother kept no more than $20,000 in any one bank, even if that meant she must have five or 10 bank accounts. She remembered the 1930s when collapsing banks were as common as falling leaves in autumn. Having each of her accounts insured by the U.S. government for $100,000 meant nothing. She needed to know that if a string of banks failed, she would not be wiped out.

I'll bet you carry vivid images of that dreadful decade even if you were born years later: soup lines; children selling apples on street corners; dust blowing over once-fertile plains; people lugging their belongings on their backs or in their cars, traveling west seeking work and better lives.

The power of the Great Depression is in its ability to alter the course of history. Just as the swollen, flooding Mississippi carves new channels in the earth, the Depression forced economic history into unforeseen paths. Our entire economic system was seriously questioned, not just in the United States, but also worldwide. Socialism and communism enjoyed popularity unknown before or since because the capitalist system was in such disarray. The Great Depression was the economic equivalent of world war—pervasive, unstoppable, devastating, and profound and with enduring consequences.

Many government institutions and policies established during that pivotal decade—Social Security, the Securities and Exchange Commission, the Federal Deposit Insurance Corporation, federal deficit spending—got their start as responses to the devastating effects of the Great Depression.

No wonder, then, that of every possible economic catastrophe that can strike us, depression, or at least serious recession, is one that is truly feared among my clients. True, a depression concerns older people more than younger ones. However, as Elvis and the Beatles are popular with kids not even alive when they were at the height of their fame, the Great Depression lives on in the consciousness of those too young to have directly suffered its effects.

As I have stated before (and it's worth repeating), I don't believe you or I will experience a Great Depression during our lifetimes, but I am not absolutely certain about that. Another depression, however unlikely, is decidedly possible. Rampaging inflation, an oil shortage, a collapse of the international monetary system due to loan defaults by Third-World countries, antagonisms brought on by trade policies, a devastating terrorist attack, a stock market bubble that bursts with such force it devastates the market, even mistakes by the Federal Reserve that make matters worse rather than relieve a future severe recession—any of these could trigger a depression or bring us deep into a severe and prolonged recession.

Yet, if I were a betting man, I'd wager that if we do have a depression, its cause would be something none of us has even thought of. In the late 1980s and early 1990s, the savings and loan industry was brought to its knees, and cost taxpayers upward of $500 billion in bailouts. Who guessed that would happen? Before October 19, 1987, "Who would have thought the stock market could fall more than 500 points in one day and nearly suffer a 'meltdown' the next?" as one New York Stock Exchange official put it: "I didn't."

Then there was September 11, 2001. Hardly anyone expected a major terrorist attack. But even more to the point, not only could we not have imagined the World Trade Center ever collapsing due to airliners crashing into them, no one imagined the devastating economic consequences of the terrorist attack. The country—and its economy—was brought to a standstill. New York City literally lost hundreds of thousands of jobs, and the country overall was affected. As devastating as the attack was on life and property, it had an effect on the psychology of our country that I never imagined I would ever see in my lifetime. Did you ever imagine our entire country entering into a kind of emotional trance that took weeks or months to get out of?

Does any reasonable American think that, at this time, we've protected our shores to a degree that another—and even possibly more traumatic and devastating terrorist attack—cannot ever again happen?

Who could have imagined such a scenario just a short time ago? All my clients carry depression protection. One reason is,

I can't accurately see into the future, nor can anyone else. In addition, I enforce the rule that all my clients have depression protection because it is free and effective and provides valuable economic and psychological benefits. And, because, quite honestly, I am not absolutely certain we won't have a depression again in our lifetimes. We may be one terrorist attack away from another 1930s scenario.

WHY WORRY ABOUT SOMETHING THAT WILL NOT HAPPEN?

We'll talk more about insurance, but it's worth noting here that the only situation one must insure against is when the probability of an event occurring is small but its consequences are catastrophic. Suppose you had to cross an open field where one land mine was planted. Though the possibility of stepping on the mine is minimal, would you take the walk unaided if someone offered you an armored car capable of withstanding a mine blast?

The armor I offer you is carefully chosen investments that ensure against a severe recession or a full-out, no-holds-barred depression. For that reason alone, having depression protection in your portfolio is a must.

Peace of mind is another great reason. Your teenager comes home late at night from a date. Even if you are sound asleep, you naturally drift into a deeper, more relaxing sleep when you hear the front door close, because you know he or she is home safe. In the same way, you may not be thinking every day about a depression, but you certainly worry about your financial future, or at least you should. The worry might be subtle, but it's there. The depression protection described here is a means of forever removing this financial worry from your concerns. It's a way of having everyone home safe.

THE LOOK OF A DEPRESSION

If a depression comes, what will it look like? No one knows. We have only the past to go by.

The Great Depression was probably worse than anyone who didn't live through it can imagine today. The production of durable goods, such as machinery and appliances (and this was a time when manufacturing was a much larger share of the economy than services, while today the opposite is true) dropped 80 percent between 1929 and the Depression's low point in March 1933. To put it another way, for every five durable goods produced in 1929, only one was produced four years later. Some examples of the sales declines that occurred between 1929 and 1933 include autos, 65 percent; railroad passenger cars, 100 percent; domestic ranges, 77 percent; and electric generators, 73 percent. The output of bicycles actually increased by 3 percent, which is not surprising considering people couldn't afford autos and gasoline.

Unemployment went from 1.5 million in 1929 to at least 13 million during the Depression's depths—an increase of more than 700 percent. Official statistics said one-quarter of the work force was out of work, but with part-timers and the under-employed, the real unemployment rate probably approached one-third. This means the average American either lived in a family without a breadwinner or had a next-door neighbor in that position.

This was at a time when Social Security, unemployment benefits and food stamps were unknown. The "safety net" created over the past seventy years did not exist in the early 1930s.

The Great Depression was the worst depression of all, though not the only one, a fact often forgotten today. Between 1920 and 1921, another depression sent the durable-goods output tumbling 43 percent. There was a depression in 1907. Before that, a depression occurred between 1893 and 1896, and another in 1873, and there were others. Sometimes they were called "panics."

In fact, the Federal Reserve Bank, or the Fed, has contingency plans for various types of economic collapse, including a depression. Clearly, they think such an event is possible. The Fed activated a prearranged plan on October 19, 1987, when the stock market crashed. The media reported the next day that the market almost disintegrated entirely and was saved with the help of the Fed's actions. That may be reassuring, but I really don't rest easier knowing the Fed has rehearsed its role if we have a depression. I would rather make my own preparations. Keep in mind, this market crash is not ancient history; it is likely remembered by most of the readers of this book.

While one can argue about the causes of depressions, no one seriously disputes the existence of economic cycles. Since the start of the Industrial Revolution and the widespread use of money, economies around the world have endured busts and booms.

A recent example has been Japan which beginning in 1990 saw a recession that persisted for over a decade. While Japan suffered, the United States had a boom period during the 1990s, only to have its economy falter at the start of the new century, including having three years of continual stock market declines (years 2000 to 2002).

Sometimes cycles don't affect entire economies but, rather, certain geographical regions. In the mid-1970s, the Northeastern United States was in a major recession, but by the mid-1980s, it was enjoying a raging boom. In the early 1990s, it was again back in a recession, only to spring out of it and do well for the remainder of that decade until 2001, when it slipped into a rut again.

Real estate goes through cycles on a geographic basis. A devastating bust immediately followed the real estate boom in Texas and Arizona from the late 1970s to the mid-1980s. A sharp downturn in California real estate in the 1990s followed a boom during the 1980s. The mid- to late-1990s saw another California real estate boom, again followed by a downturn, especially in Silicon Valley when the technology boom turned to bust. As I write this, California is going through another real estate boom.

Some call this phenomenon a *rolling recession*, where economic doldrums strike one region before moving on. Although no widely accepted definition of a depression exists, it is an uncommonly severe, devastating economic period, going beyond the dislocations and difficulties found in a recession.

There have been economic cycles in this country basically since its founding, and certainly since the latter half of the 19th century when it started to develop a major industrial economy. These include downturns that cause widespread hardships, such as those all of us have seen in our own time. Before I die, I'm sure I'll see a few more. Whether any of these will lead to a depression is anyone's guess, but every downturn has the potential to snowball out of control into a severe recession or depression.

OUR MODEL

The ambiguous nature of a future depression means that we have to make assumptions about what it would be like in order to plan effectively. Anyone can argue with assumptions, but I base mine on experiences our nation endured during the Great Depression and what I see as potential problems if another depression strikes.

What are some problems? First, poor sales and profits could close the doors of many major corporations. The heavy debt burden so many companies assumed during the easy-money days of the past couple of decades could destroy many others. Servicing debt—paying the monthly interest—will be impossible for many companies, because a company's debt has to be paid, without regard to how well or poorly the company is performing financially.

These big-business failures, if they occur, will have widespread economic implications. The pension plans millions of Americans are counting on for retirement could be wiped out. Government regulations, like the Employee Retirement Income Security Act (ERISA), try to protect pension plans by insuring that pension money is wisely and securely invested. However, in a period of great economic uncertainty, even these plans won't emerge unscathed. ERISA, for instance, considers investments in stocks and bonds to be secure, yet these are the very financial instruments likely to suffer losses in a depression. The corporate bonds many rely on for income will become virtually worthless. After all, it is this debt, in addition to market conditions, that will cause businesses to fail in the first place. Even insured bank accounts will be in trouble because the Federal Insurance Deposit Corporation won't be able to cover the obligations of all the failed banks.

The stock market will head south as sure as birds do each winter. Standard & Poor's 500 Stock Composite Index's high in 1929 was 31.92. It got as low as 4.40 in 1932, a drop in value of more than 86 percent. Had you invested $10,000 in a representative sample of the S&P stocks at the 1929 high, three years later your investment would have hit a low of $1,378.45. Between 1931 and 1939, the S&P never went higher than 18.68 (in 1937) and most of the time was in the range of 8 to 13. In fact, the S&P took 25 years to recover from the Depression. Not until 1954 did it top its 1929 high.

In a typical depression, hard assets, especially real estate, get clobbered. Farm property dropped 37 percent in value between 1929 and 1933, at the same time commercial property values fell by about a third.

Think this can't happen again? Well, in recent history we haven't quite duplicated the stock market meltdown of the 1930s, but we've come close, especially if one looks at the tech-heavy NASDAQ Composite index. It was at 5,133 on March 10, 2000. About two and a half years later (31 months to be exact), October 9, 2002, this index was at 1,136. That's a drop of 78 percent—versus the 89 percent the Dow dropped from its 1929 high of 381 to its 1932 low of 41, and the period of time for the two meltdowns was almost identical. We are not immune today to the stock market, or at least significant parts of it, disintegrating. We've all seen it happen very, very recently. The year-end values for the NASDAQ composite index over the 20 year period beginning in 1986 is shown in Figure 4. You will notice that the down slope is almost exactly the same as the upslope. This clearly shows that when a market goes up like a rocket, it comes down like a rock. Always keep that in mind while investing.

Based on all this, my model of the depression consists of the following assumptions:

1. Prices will decline 35 percent, minimum (probably more).

2. Interest rates will drop to 1 percent (they dropped *below* 1 percent during the 1930s and are between 1 and 2 percent as I write this—a percentage rate that, five years ago or so, was inconceivable).

3. Social Security and private pension plans will provide minimal income; so minimal it probably won't be worth talking about.

Figure 4: Nasdaq Composite Index

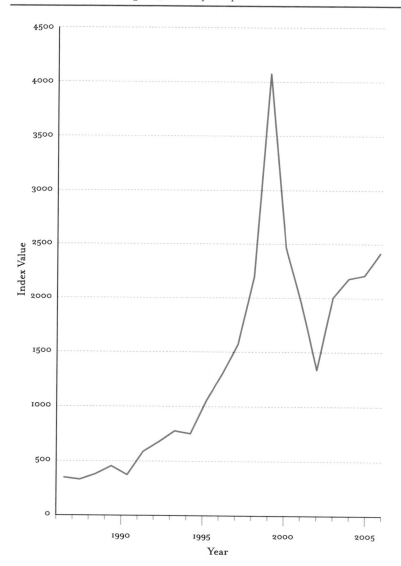

4. The value of stocks, bonds and hard assets will fall pre-
   cipitously by 75 percent or more.

This is scary stuff, but I think I'm being conservative.

DEPRESSION PROTECTION: TREASURY BONDS

With this picture, what's left that's worth investing in? Quite
simply, U.S. Treasury bonds, commonly called Treasuries—the
money the U.S. government borrows every day and for which it
pays reasonable interest. (Note: I'm referring to Treasuries,
which pay a fixed rate of interest, which is most of them; those
that pay a variable rate should not be used for Bulletproofing.)

Treasury bonds are like other bonds, except they are issued
and backed by the federal government, and the interest they pay
is not taxable for state income tax purposes, but is taxed for federal income tax purposes. Bonds are simply a way for a government agency or company to borrow money. That makes the
investor a lender to the government or company. The power of
Treasury bonds comes from the fact that bond prices increase
as interest rates fall, all other things being equal. The reason for
the inverse relationship between bond prices and interest rate
is explained in a later chapter.

In a world of declining prices, as happens in a depression
or severe recession, bond prices theoretically should go through
the roof, "all other things being equal," as economists love to
say. But in the real world, all other things are rarely equal, and
they certainly aren't for bonds during an economic calamity,
hence the second reason I recommend Treasury bonds: Of all
bonds issued during a depression, the *only* ones certain to pay
their interest are those issued by the U.S. government. Today's
high-grade corporate bonds may not be worth much more than
the stock of these companies—nearly nothing—because even

major corporations will have enormous difficulties paying their debts, which includes paying you, the bondholder, interest for borrowing your money and paying you back the principal or face value of the bond when it falls due. So, even if interest rates fall, no one will pay more for corporate bonds because the likelihood of collecting the interest is slight. In fact, bond prices (of bonds other than Treasuries) will probably fall, rather than rise, even while interest rates plummet.

Treasury bonds will pay for one reason—the government controls the printing presses, making it impossible for the government to run out of money. Sending you, the bondholder, money is easy—it just means having the printing presses run a little longer.

True, the government can do the same to meet Social Security and unemployment obligations, but those are defined by legislation that Congress can change quickly. Congress will cut Social Security and other benefits rather than risk the sustained inflation that printing more and more money brings on.

Congress enjoys no such power over bonds. If the government borrows $1,000 via a 30-year bond and promises to pay 9 percent per annum, that obligation cannot be changed without the government going into default. U.S. government debt obligations are the safest investments *in the world* precisely because everyone believes the government's promise to pay.

Here we touch on one of the paradoxes of the economic world: As much as we'd like to believe that economies rise and fall on the cold, immutable laws of mathematics, in truth the messy world of human emotion intrudes here, too. Why people believe the U.S. government will always pay its debts, even if it means printing money to do so, is like asking why the sun rises in the east. So far, it always has, and tomorrow and every day thereafter, there's no reason to think it will do otherwise.

For Treasury bonds, then, it is really a question of confidence. People have more confidence in the ability of the U.S.

government to repay its debts and so are willing to buy these bonds, especially in uncertain times. Partly because of this on-going cash infusion based on confidence, the government is, in fact, always able to pay its debts, living on to borrow another day. To you, the investor, the bottom line is that the government will run its printing presses into the ground before reneging on its obligations.

Now, what happens if you have a 30-year Treasury bond yielding 9 percent? Let's assume you bought the bond five years before the depression when things looked good (remember that before October 29, 1929, few people saw a major depression coming, and before March 2000, few saw the collapse of technology (and other) stocks, so don't expect a lot of warning signs). The bond has 25 years left to maturity. When the depression hits, interest rates fall to 1 percent.

Most bonds are traded freely across their term, meaning you don't have to hold your $1,000, 30-year bond for 30 years; you can sell it, even at a loss (for an amount less than $1,000), at any time if you have a buyer. The bond's market value changes over time, too. Initially, the biggest factor affecting the bond's value is interest rates. When a bond is almost mature, however, its value reverts to the redemption value since the period of time it has left to pay interest to the holder is so short.

When interest rates across the market fall (say to 1 percent, 8 percentage points less than your bond pays), the market value of the bond goes up and vice versa. This is because someone wanting to buy a bond that would have an equivalent value at maturity would, of course, have to pay more initially to make up for the 8 percentage-point fall in interest rates. In this case, a $1,000, 30-year bond paying 9 percent interest has the same value as a $2,765.71 bond paying 1 percent interest, which means that quite suddenly your $1,000 bond paying 9 percent is worth (given a buyer) $2,765.71. (This calculation, by the way, is a *future value* calculation.)

Let's now look at depression-proofing your whole portfolio, which we'll say is worth $100,000 before the depression. What is important is to have enough assets during a depression so that no purchasing power is lost compared with what you have today.

My model assumes that prices decline 35 percent, based on what occurred in the 1930s. This means a bond worth $2,765.71 during a future depression will buy $4,254.94 worth of goods and services in today's dollars since what once cost $1 now costs 65 cents. (This is done with simple arithmetic: 1 − 0.35 divided into $2,765.71.) Why does the value go up as prices decline? Because the more prices drop, the more you can buy with each dollar you have.

Say when you bought the bond, movie tickets cost $10 for adults and $6 for children. Taking your family to the movies—you, your spouse and your two children—cost $32. When the depression hit, movie theaters lowered their prices 35 percent: $10 movie tickets now cost $6.50, $6 movie tickets cost $3.90. The total cost for you and your family at the movies: $20.80. That's $11.20 less than what you used to pay for the same outing. Assume you buy popcorn for $6.20 and drinks for $5. The evening still costs $32, but now you're getting popcorn and drinks for the same money that before only bought tickets. In the same way, the value of bonds increase (you can buy more) as prices decline.

The bond cost you $1,000, so for every $1 of cost, you have got about $4.25 worth of buying power. This provides us with a multiplier of 4.25. Every dollar invested today in a Treasury bond, if a depression hits, will buy $4.25 worth of goods and services.

If about $23,500 of your $100,000 in assets are in long-term Treasury bonds and a depression comes, the purchasing power of those bonds becomes $100,000 (4.25 × $23,500). You are completely covered in that your ability to buy $100,000 of goods and services in today's dollars has not declined; the difference is made up by the enhanced value of your bond.

In the real world, though, you wouldn't need to put so much into Treasuries because your other assets, although less valuable, will almost certainly be worth something. Let's say you put $80,000 of your assets in non-depression-protection assets such as stocks or real estate, and during a depression, the value of those assets falls 75 percent. What was worth $80,000 is now worth only $20,000. Because we're assuming prices fall 35 percent, these assets can now buy, in today's dollars, $30,769.31 worth of goods and services. With this $30,000 or so, you need additional assets worth about $70,000 in purchasing power to make you whole. Since our multiplier is 4.25, you need $16,470.59 in depression-protection assets. The assets you buy with this $16,000+ are Treasury bonds.

Looked at from another angle, with a little over 16 percent of your portfolio invested in 30-year Treasury bonds, your net worth is *completely protected against a depression*. And this protection is free. Why? Because Treasury bonds are an excellent investments even if we never have a depression. However, recognize that during periods of high inflation, such as we had in the late 1970s and early 1980s, Treasury bonds, like all fixed-income investments, lose value as prices increase. As prices rise, the value of the interest paid by the bonds declines. To counter inflation, we use investments that increase in value with rising prices, which are discussed in the next chapter. No matter what you think of the likelihood of a depression occurring, you need Treasuries in your portfolio because of their safety and their yield. Their depression protection is a welcomed bonus.

Another caveat: Don't make the mistake of thinking you are protected by investing in a government-bond mutual fund (or annuity), which is a mutual fund that invests exclusively (or nearly so) in government bonds. The longer the length of maturity of a bond, the more protection it affords. Fund managers sometimes have short- to medium-term investment horizons, such as 5 or 10 years. That's a lot shorter than the 30-year bonds I recommend you buy.

Another major shortcoming of government-bond mutual funds is that when the bond market fluctuates (which it certainly will in a depression), fund managers will likely sell off their bonds. Managers will act this way because the prices of the bonds will rise and the managers, to make their track records look good, will want to lock in profits—to have the money in hand so to speak. It's an approach exactly opposite from what I recommend, which is buy and *hold*. The only time you sell in the depths of a depression is if you absolutely need the money to live on. By the time we get into the deepest trough of a depression, I predict most fund managers will have largely sold out and will be holding cash. Though the value of those dollars will increase as prices decline, it won't compare to the increase in values we'll see with Treasuries.

DEPRESSION PROTECTION: STRIPS

Besides buying Treasuries directly, another financial instrument also provides superb depression protection, namely, strips. A *strip* is a long-term, say, 30-year Treasury bond that an investment banking firm has stripped of its interest. They sell at prices heavily discounted from their face value.

Before everything was electronic, bonds were printed pieces of paper. Along the bond's edge were small coupons, each of which represented an interest payment. Each six months or whenever the interest fell due, the bondholder would clip the coupon, take it to a bank, and redeem it for the interest due. This is all done electronically today. When you think of strips, picture the investment banking firm stripping, or clipping, off all the interest coupons and keeping them for itself and selling you just the bond without interest.

Why would anyone want to buy a bond that pays no interest? First, the bond itself has value because when it matures, it can be redeemed for its face value. Second, because the bond doesn't pay interest, the investment-banking firm sells the bond at a steep discount from the face value. The difference between the bond's face value and what you pay is calculated so that it represents (surprise!) the market's prevailing rate of interest. There's nothing unusual about this arrangement. After all, the ever-popular U.S. EE Savings Bonds are strips; they don't pay interest periodically but sell at a steep discount from their face value. Strips and EE Savings Bonds also are called *zero-coupon bonds,* because they do not have coupons.

Assume you buy a $1,000 30-year strip for $75.37. The imputed rate of interest of this bond is 9 percent, the prevailing interest rate. Five years later, a depression is raging. Based on interest rates having fallen to 1 percent and with accrued interest, the bond is now worth $779.77 (calculated as we saw earlier by using future values).

Assuming prices have dropped 35 percent, the purchasing power of that $779.77 bond based on the present value of the dollar is $1,199.65. (To calculate this number, take 1 minus the percentage drop in value, or 0.35, which comes to 0.65, and divide this into the present value, which is $779.77.) The bottom line is, you invest $75.37 and get $1,199.65 in depression protection. That's a multiple of 15.92. For every dollar you invest, you receive $15.92 worth of depression protection.

With about 6 percent of your portfolio invested in strips, your net worth is fully protected. This supposes the unlikely event that the value of the remainder of your portfolio drops to zero. Assuming the rest of your portfolio drops 75 percent, you can fully protect yourself against a depression by devoting less than 5 percent of your portfolio to strips.

However, there are disadvantages to strips compared to conventional Treasury bonds. Because strips don't provide a stream of income (Treasuries pay the interest every six months), you don't get any cash from your investment until the strip matures. Also, even though you get zero cash until the bond's maturity, you have to pay taxes on accumulated interest every year. So, not only do strips not provide any cash flow, they actually create negative cash flow. Placing the strips in a tax-deferred account, such as an individual retirement account (IRA), postpones the tax liability.

Strips also are more volatile than Treasury bonds, which makes some investors nervous. The volatility is not because investors are concerned about their quality (these are, after all, government securities), but because strips reflect changes in interest rates only through their prices. Conventional bonds are not quite as volatile because, no matter what their prices, bondholders know they will get a stream of guaranteed income; their only volatility comes in the market price of the bond should they want to sell any time before maturity. The situation is similar to stocks. Growth stocks, which rarely pay dividends but have considerable growth potential (meaning, there's a good chance their price will increase), are more volatile than utility stocks, which typically pay sizable dividends but change slowly in value, if at all.

Volatility is *good*. The more volatile the bond, the more depression protection it provides. If the economy goes into a tailspin and the investment hardly responds, then it provides little protection. Only when the investment responds strongly, such as with a strip, do you get significant protection. Strips provide lots of bang for the buck—much protection for little investment—precisely because they are so volatile. The volatility is not an issue of risk because you won't even consider selling the strips unless there's a depression. You sell only when the condition for which the investment was bought occurs, such as a depression. In the long run, volatility will have zero effect on your strips' value, and you'll get the guaranteed return at maturity. When it comes to that part of your investment portfolio providing depression and inflation protection, volatility is your friend. The remainder of your portfolio is where your growth happens.

The type of security best for you—Treasuries bonds or strips—depends on your need for cash and the risk you are prepared to take over a certain span of time. (Risk is discussed in detail in Chapter 6.) Conservative investors usually go with Treasuries. They like the cash flow and the low volatility, and the secure, conservative nature of Treasuries is appealing, even discounting their protection characteristics.

Investors that are more adventurous go for strips, which allow them to devote a greater percentage of their portfolio to other investments. Other investments are, by definition, more aggressive because every investment is riskier than U.S. government obligations. Many investors take part of their portfolio and devote it to growth stocks and other higher-potential/higher-risk investments. They don't want to have too much of their money tied up in government securities.

Sometimes, investors have their money tied up in illiquid assets (the harder it is to turn an asset into cash, the more "illiquid" it is), such as real estate or annuities, and it is hard for them to come up with the cash to buy Treasuries equal to 15 percent or so of their portfolio's value. However, few people have so many illiquid investments that they can't get 5 percent of their holdings in cash. Using strips, this 5 percent provides very adequate depression protection.

An Example

One day, a potential client came into my office. Like most people, he came to me with virtually no depression protection. He had recently gotten a 65-page financial plan from one of the largest and oldest national financial planning firms in the country. Its cost: $800. Its value: $0. The plan was so complex that it was practically beyond comprehension. Further, its recommendations were so difficult to implement that it was not worth the time and expense required. The ongoing cost of tracking a complex portfolio was an additional factor, too. In desperation, he came to me.

In this analysis, like all others, I include only investment assets, not assets for personal use, such as the house one lives in. I assume that use of personal assets will continue in the same way whether or not there is an economic catastrophe.

Briefly, he had about $19,000 in cash and CDs, money he could get his hands on quickly. There was another $16,000 or so in corporate bonds and about $24,000 in stocks and stock mutual funds. A piece of undeveloped land was worth $20,000, and he had another $50,000 tied up in a limited partnership. All this added up to $129,000. But the bulk of his estate was in a fixed annuity (an annuity that guarantees repayment of the principal) worth $139,000. (Oh, the persuasiveness of insurance salespeople who sell these annuities that are such poor investments.) Because fixed-income annuities are debt instruments issued by the insurance company, they are equivalent only to low-grade corporate bonds: The value of both depends on the ability of private organizations to repay their debt during times of financial upheaval (annuities are discussed in detail in Chapter 9).

What was his problem? He had virtually no depression protection. The annuity, though secure in normal times, would drop dramatically in value during a depression because the insurance company wouldn't be able to pay it. Insurance companies can pay interest on their annuities—the "income"—because of the returns they earn on other investments. Those other investments, however, are real estate and corporate stocks and bonds, which may plummet in value in a depression. It's a safe bet that insurance companies will be in deep trouble during a depression (as in 1929) and policyholders will be left holding the bag. My advice to him—and to you: Don't count much on your insurance policies if we get into a depression.

He had another common problem. Most of his investments were illiquid; it was hard for him to turn these investments into ready cash. He could get cash from the annuity, for instance, only on a slow piecemeal basis of 10 percent a year. Turning the limited partnership and real estate into cash was also difficult and would be significantly more so in a severe downturn.

As a result, I advised him to place 5 percent of his assets in Treasury strips this year and 5 percent in Treasury bonds next year. His entire estate was worth about $258,000, so 5 percent meant coming up with about $13,000 in cash. With his savings account and CD, that was not a problem the first year. With only $13,000 in strips, he handled his small tax liability easily. The following year would be soon enough to start liquidating some of his illiquid assets, such as the annuity and limited partnership, so he wouldn't have to tap into cash reserves to raise this second $13,000. Because he was putting money into Treasury bonds, there was a positive cash flow, which helped pay the taxes on the strips.

Most important, he was protected against a depression. I used a conservative 15 multiple for the strips and a 4 multiple for the Treasury bonds. Every dollar he invested in a strip would be worth $15 in the event of a depression. The strips would have a value of $195,000 and the bonds, $52,000, for a total of $247,000. Since his current portfolio was worth $258,000, this left his protection $11,000 short, which the value of his remaining portfolio would easily cover.

Here was a man who had virtually no depression protection and few liquid assets. Yet, with a couple of simple easy-to-implement investments, I could protect him from a depression while putting him into investments that provided excellent returns with a high degree of safety. He's since thrown away his useless 65-page financial plan and now sleeps soundly.

DEPRESSION-PROTECTION PORTFOLIO BASICS

We'll learn in detail all about risk and how it relates to you in Chapter 6, but here are some simple guidelines:

- *Low-risk.* If you are a low-risk investor, the investments of choice are 30-year Treasuries or plain cash. These are low risk because they don't involve leverage (borrowed money or debt), are sure to pay interest and are less volatile than long-term Treasuries. About 35 percent of your portfolio should be in Treasury bills (one year or less to maturity) or 17 percent in 30-year Treasury bonds.

- *Medium-risk.* Medium-risk investors should put 4 percent of their portfolio in Treasury bills and 10 percent in Treasury bonds.

- *High-risk.* Aggressive, high-risk investors can put 7 percent in strips (in fact, 6 percent is adequate but the asset allocation model uses 7 percent). Strips have a low risk of default, but they are volatile, which usually makes low- and medium-risk investors nervous. That's why these are recommended only for high-risk investors. Strips can provide all the depression protection you need.

A RECAP

In a depression:

- Hard assets, such as real estate and gold, will lose much of their value.

- Stocks will lose much of their value.
- Prices will decline.
- Interest rates will decline.

As a result:

- In a depression, the only investments that are sure to increase in value are U.S. government securities.
- The losses incurred in one's investments during a depression can be offset by the gains of long-term U.S. government securities.

INFLATION BULLETPROOFING

MAKE YOUR MONEY LAST AS LONG AS YOU DO

> If you want safety in an unsafe world . . .
>
> If you want to make sure your money is there when you need it . . .
>
> If you want to fight inflation and the devaluation of the dollar . . .
>
> **You need to read this chapter.**

"The sins of the fathers are to be laid upon the children," Shakespeare wrote. He wasn't referring to inflation, which is a rise in the general level of prices, but he could have been. It's not uncommon today for children to find their parents have committed the "sin" of lacking enough retirement money, with inflation being the culprit. Single-handedly, it erodes one's retirement income and either the children have to pick up the slack or one has to do without. It's like the effects of too much sunshine: It accumulates and accumulates and eventually it can cause cancer. This is what happens with inflation. It accumulates and accumulates, and eventually it sickens your retirement nest egg to the point where it can no longer support you the way you had hoped.

> **The Really Stupid: Not factoring in inflation when setting up your retirement finances.**

Professionals Joan and Mark have three children. Their incomes are good, but they came to me to gain better control of their finances. As we discussed their financial situation, I innocently asked if they had any dependents besides their children. That's when I heard the harrowing story of Joan's parents. Her father, employed by the same firm all his working life, retired with what seemed to be an adequate pension. Adding Social Security, their financial future was secure. Or so they thought.

Joan's father retired in the late 1970s when inflation was building steam. Within five years, Joan's parents saw their expenses increase nearly 70 percent. At the same time, their income increased a mere 20 percent, which came entirely from Social Security cost-of-living adjustments since the pension payout was fixed. When I spoke with Joan and Mark, they were responsible for keeping a roof over the heads and food on the table of Joan's parents. Her parents had become entirely dependent, financially, on Joan and Mark.

Were Joan's parents profligate? Unwise with their investments? Unconcerned with their future? The answer is no. Their spending was responsible; they invested conservatively and planned thoroughly for their future. In a sense they suffered from something they never dreamed about: bad luck.

They were unlucky because they began their retirement when inflation was dramatically increasing. Inflation—at *any* level—can be devastating. At a 6 percent annual inflation rate, prices *double* in 12 years and *triple* in 19. If inflation is raging at 12 percent, prices double in seven short years and triple in 10.

Let's say inflation rolls along at about 3 percent a year. Be aware that a mere 3 percent inflation rate can still be devastating over the long run. At this rate, prices double in 24 years. If you are now 60 years old and starting retirement, when you hit 84 (which probably most of today's 60-year-olds will do), every dollar you have will lose half its earning power. You won't have to wait until age 84 to feel the effects of inflation. At a 3 per-

cent annual inflation rate, you will lose 10 percent of your buying power in four short years, and 20 percent in seven years. A
20-percent drop in your income is significant and could start
you on the path of the destruction of your retirement assets by
forcing you to eat some of the seed corn.

The older you are, the more inflation is likely to affect you.
This is because the cost of health care tends to rise faster than
the overall inflation rate. The older you are, the greater the
percentage of your income will be spent on health care. Since
you will probably spend more and more money on healthcare
as you age, and healthcare will become increasingly expensive,
inflation is likely to hit you harder than younger folks.

Think of inflation as being similar to radiation. A little X-
ray radiation now and then causes no harm. Over a lifetime, radiation damage builds up in the body. It never goes away. Too
many doses, even if each is small, can cause serious problems,
even death.

INFLATION

Exactly what is inflation? George W. Wilson, in his book,
Inflation: Causes, Consequences and Cures, states that inflation is "the
persistent rise in the *general* level of prices" [his emphasis]. Re-
searchers claim to have found evidence of inflation as far back
as ancient Greece and Rome, so it is nothing new.

What really constitutes inflation and at what level rising
prices begin to be seen as "high" inflation is open to interpretation. Personal values and experience color our perceptions of
it. In the 1950s and 1960s, inflation was perhaps about 2 percent. For much of the 1970s, it was 6 percent. Then President
Nixon instituted wage and price controls in the early 1970s because inflation seemed to be getting out of control—it was about
6 percent at the time. Barely 10 years later, most economists

would hardly raise an eyebrow at similar price increases. Between 1978 and 1981, the inflation rate was between 10 and 12 percent per year! During the 1980s, the inflation rate moved down to the 4 to 5 percent range, and in the 1990s and early 2000s, it stayed more in the 2 to 3 percent range.

Could double-digit inflation happen again? Of course, there's no question about it. Is it likely? Perhaps not, at least not any time soon, though I can't say I would be surprised to see a sustained period of high inflation 20 or 30 years from now. That seems very possible, though I'm not sure it is probable.

However, it seems nearly every week there are articles about inflation. They address such issues as the threat of inflation, the actions of the Federal Reserve in response to inflation concerns, the rise in prices this month versus last month or last year, et al. For several years now, the media has been filled with stories about inflation—at a time when inflation was a low 2 or 3 percent. Why the interest? Because no matter the current inflation rate, inflation is a long-term concern. There's no getting around it, inflation remains a threat to all of us. Here's a prediction I want to make: For as long as anyone now reading this book is alive, inflation will be a concern. Sometimes it will be more of a concern than at others, but it will *always* be a concern. Inflation will never—can never—be whipped. It always will be with us.

What's important is not whether we run into a stretch of foul economic weather, but that we wear the protective clothing needed if we do.

It is more difficult to create a Bulletproofing model for inflation than recession. There has never been hyper or even sustained severe inflation in this country, so we have no history to go by. Inflation-protection investments are also more varied than those for depression. In addition, the price fluctuations of such investments over time are more difficult to calculate. Bond prices, for instance, move in fairly predictable ways when interest rates move. That's not true of real estate prices during inflation, though it is true that *real estate is the most effective hedge against inflation.* Though prices for inflation investments are relatively unpredictable, certain parameters can be constructed that help us create inflation-protection portfolios.

THE INFLATION SCENARIO

If we have severe inflation, I see the value of certain investments increasing *faster* than the inflation rate. If inflation turns into real hyperinflation, say 100 percent or more a year, the investments I recommend will work remarkably well. In fact, the higher the inflation rate, the better protection these investments provide. You actually need fewer of these investments if inflation goes bananas because these recommendations skyrocket in value with price increases.

The reason for this is that the values of certain investments, such as commercial real estate, go up at an increasing rate as inflation builds up steam. I estimate certain inflation-protection investments, which I'll discuss shortly, will increase at the following annual rates:

Inflation rate of 10 percent: Inflation-protection investments increase 13 percent.

Inflation rate of 20 percent: Inflation-protection investments increase 30 percent.

Inflation rate of 100 percent: Inflation-protection investments increase 200 percent.

Here's an example. You buy a piece of commercial real estate for $250,000. For the five years after your purchase, inflation runs at 10 percent a year. When inflation is at this rate, we expect inflation-protection investments, like commercial real estate, to increase 13 percent annually. By the end of Year 5, your property is worth a bit over $460,000, but in real buying terms (the original worth of money in Year 1 dollars); it is worth $286,000 or about 14 percent more than you originally paid for it.

At 14 percent for the five years, or about 2.7 percent (again, in real terms), you haven't made much money. You have, however, more than kept up with inflation, which is quite an accomplishment in itself.

The arithmetic looks like this:

First year: $250,000 × 1.13 = $282,500
Second year: $282,500 × 1.13 = $319,225
Third year: $319,225 × 1.13 = $360,724
Fourth year: $360,724 × 1.13 = $407,618
Fifth year: $407,618 × 1.13 = $460,609

Since prices have gone up 10 percent a year, $460,609 just doesn't buy what it used to. $460,609 at the end of Year 5 can buy what $286,002 could buy at the beginning of Year 1 (this is calculated by discounting the 10 percent a year that prices increased). This discounted figure of $286,002 is $36,002 more than you started with.

If inflation jumps to 20 percent a year, we expect commercial real estate to appreciate 30 percent annually. By the end of Year 5, it has a nominal value of $928,000. What is this $928,000 worth in real terms? Since prices increased 20 percent a year, it buys what $373,000 could at the beginning of Year 1. That's an increase in *real value* of about 50 percent over your initial $250,000 investment (this is calculated by discounting the 20 percent a year that prices increased). You could now buy commercial real estate worth $373,000 (in present dollars) without any additional strain on your finances.

What accounts for the power of certain investments to increase in value? Is this smoke-and-shadows created by economists *cum* magicians? The most important reason hard assets increase faster than inflation is the famed economic law of supply and demand.

As inflation surges, those with money in other places—bonds, stocks, money market accounts, CDs, mutual funds—find their rates of return fixed or at best unable to keep up with inflation, so they bail out. They make a beeline to the dollar signs. The supply of hard assets remains the same while the demand for them dramatically increases. Real estate, gold and other hard assets attract the attention of the cash-rich, and they practically throw money at these investments.

The greater the inflation rate, the more investors will want to jump on the hard-asset bandwagon. Their actions amplify the increase in prices of these investments, pushing them up faster than inflation, which just attracts even more investors and more money. The United States has always been a safe haven for money, a place where money flows to when times are bad in other countries. It is conceivable that there might be a flight of capital from the United States to other nations in such high-inflation times, but I think it unlikely. Americans have never acted this way, though, admittedly, there's always a first time. More importantly, if the United States is experiencing runaway inflation, much of the rest of the world probably is as well.

Note that investment advisors, stockbrokers, financial planners often say you should hold stocks to protect against inflation. Over time, stocks have gone up more than inflation; that is true. But during highly inflationary times, with corporate profits weak and people looking for something tangible to invest in, stock prices tend to go down. Also, stocks are competing against CDs, bonds and other financial assets that provide guaranteed returns. As the returns on these go up, the appeal of stocks goes down.

These investors aren't being stupid. Money market accounts, bonds, stocks, and the like just can't keep up with full-speed-ahead inflation.

Pension plans frequently lack inflation investments, nor are they usually indexed to inflation, leaving those dependent on such pension plans financially ravaged when inflation is high, and even badly hurt when inflation is relatively moderate. Most importantly, they seldom make real estate available so that you can hedge inflation. Again, let me say that real estate is the most effective hedge against inflation.

Social Security is also problematical. At best, its price adjustments always lag by one year since they are calculated on what the Consumer Price Index did the *previous* 12 months. If inflation runs at 10 percent a year, this lag time seriously affects the buying power of Social Security payments. A severe period of inflation may even force Congress to curtail the Social Security cost-of-living adjustment for fear of bankrupting the whole system. As I write this, there is constant talk about limiting Social Security payments, privatizing investments in Social Security, the prospect of Social Security going bankrupt and more.

The last word is that tangible assets with inherent value, like real estate, will always have value. You can live in your house; you can't live in your mutual fund. Viewed in this light, the flight of capital to assets with tangible values makes a lot of sense. And this is what happens when inflation begins to pick up speed.

BULLETPROOF YOUR PORTFOLIO AGAINST INFLATION

Bulletproofing your portfolio against inflation involves a basket of investments. These include:

Real Estate

For most people, real estate, in the form of a home, is their largest one-time expense. Many mistakenly view their home as their largest *investment;* a home is not an investment because it is for personal use, not for generating income or capital gains.

You have to live somewhere, so even if you sell your home, you'll have to pay rent rather than use the money for nonhousing purchases. The assets you accumulate for retirement will likely be your largest investment.

Real estate does well during inflation periods, and in some years when inflation has been low in part to price fluctuations in other markets, real estate is left as one of the few buyable investments at a given time. According to the Office of Federal Housing Enterprise Oversight, a federal government agency, housing appreciated nationwide 11.17 percent in 2004, 49.67 percent for the five-year period of 2000 to 2004, and 240.69 percent since 1980. The inflation rate for 2004 was 2.75 percent, about one-quarter (25 percent) the rate at which housing prices increased. From January 2000 to December 2004, inflation was 12.74 percent, again about one quarter the rate at which housing prices increased.

During the first four years of the decade beginning in 2000, real estate was the best performing asset class of all. The reason for this was that real estate was ignored during the 1990s in favor of the high-tech market, so prices were very low. As a result, when the high-tech bubble burst, real estate was one of the few investments that did well. Note: during the three down years consisting of 2000, 2001 and 2002, *all* of the protection investments we used in our portfolios did well.

Of course, prices don't move in synch around the country. For the years 2000 to 2004, when the national average was about 50 percent, the District of Columbia saw the greatest increase, 112.13 percent, and California had the second largest gain at 102.35, while at the bottom sat Utah, 16.17 percent and Indiana, 20.02 percent. During the 25 years of 1980 to 2004, when the national gain was about 240 percent, Massachusetts had the biggest gain, 574.83 percent, followed by New York's 458.22 percent. At the low end were Oklahoma, 80.61 percent, and Texas, 94.79 percent. Real estate prices, unlike stock or gold prices, are very local.

Over the long run, real estate generally does quite well. In fact, Peter S. Spiro, in his book, *Real Interest Rates and Investment and Borrowing Strategy,* claims "there is . . . no perfect hedge against inflation, but real estate . . . appears to be the best of the alternatives."

Lack of liquidity is real estate's most important shortcoming, for it cannot be converted quickly into cash. Stocks and bonds are far more liquid: Call up your broker or go to your broker's website and they are almost immediately sold and you have your money within days. That's liquidity (the easier an asset is to turn into cash, the "more liquid" it is said to be). I'm referring here to directly buying real estate. You can invest in real estate via real estate investment trusts, which trade on the New York Stock Exchange, that invest in real estate and are highly liquid. But if you buy a piece of real estate, recognize it is not a very liquid asset.

For some people, though, illiquidity is an important advantage. If the market disintegrates and they panic and want to sell, they're stuck. They have to hold onto their property until the market turns up because as badly as they want to sell, there are no buyers in a really bad real estate market. This forces them to continue to hold the property. By then, they have weathered the worst of the market and can earn a decent return on their investment. This makes the real estate market a nearly perfect investment regulator—it lets you sell when the market's high and practically prevents you from selling when it's low.

The Good: You can control a lot of real estate with a little bit of money.

Real estate's leverage potential is a bonus to the investor. This refers to your ability to multiply the amount of property that can be bought by using credit; if you have $100,000 for a 20 percent down payment, you can borrow the rest to purchase $500,000 worth of property. As little as nothing down can get you a piece of property, but most of the time you are going to need at least 5 percent to 10 percent down. This way you can control real estate worth 5 to 10 times the amount of money you have on hand. During times of inflation, this advantage becomes even greater because you are paying off your mortgages with "cheaper" dollars that are less valuable because of inflation.

It also offers tax advantages, such as writing off the interest paid on real estate purchased for investment purposes and deducting depreciation if your income is below $100,000. This is one of the few tax shelters left to the moderate-income earner. One never knows what Congress will do with tax laws, but at the time of this writing, real estate offers some decided tax advantages.

Real estate's advantages during inflation are:

- Its value increases faster than the general price level.
- It can be bought in a variety of ways.
- Leveraging is easy.
- It has tax benefits no matter what inflation is doing.

The Stupid: You can control a lot of real estate with a little bit of money.

Having a lot of real estate can be stupid in times when inflation isn't high. Your investment in real estate can be wiped out with a very small decrease in prices and you have to pay the interest payments on real estate that may be more than you can handle over the-long term. Always make sure when you buy real estate that you can handle any potential negative cash flow if you have vacancies or raw land.

Gold

Another classic inflation-protection investment is gold. When the economy does well and inflation is moderate, as during the 1980s, gold tends not to perform well. However, it can be a strong hedge when the economy falters because of high inflation. Gold also did really well in the wake of the 9/11 terrorist attacks. It went up 20 percent, and the gold stock mutual fund that I liked best at that time, First Eagle Gold Fund, went up 160 percent. So using a gold stock mutual fund as a hedge against another 9/11-type attack or inflation provides a little more leverage than gold itself. It's also a little easier to sell or buy because you don't have to lug around heavy bars of gold.

The Good: Gold is a hedge against fear. Whatever horrible events may befall the United States or the world, people flock to gold. Having gold as part of your portfolio will help make up for any huge drops in the stock market during some types of crisis.

When choosing a gold stock mutual fund, make sure that it is a fund that in the past has not bought gold mining stocks that sell options on their future production. When gold skyrockets or takes a jump, the gold stock mutual funds that have sold options on their future production will be selling gold at a low price, even though the price may have gone up 10 times. Whereas, those that haven't sold options on their future production provide a purer play on the price of gold and the gold stock mutual fund increases much more, as a result.

Gold is perhaps history's oldest and most enduring investment vehicle. For thousands of years, people have bought,

hoarded, traded, hidden and coveted gold. The Spanish con-
quistadors came to the New World to find gold. The glittering
metal has long held a fascination for people around the world
exceeded only by their passion for religion, politics and possibly love.

Mary, my client who grew up during the Great Depression,
learned to appreciate gold at an early age. Her father always kept
gold bullion coins for a rainy day. Over time, as his wealth increased, he increased his holdings. He had a hoard when President Nixon, in 1971, set the price of gold free. Overnight, gold
jumped from $35 an ounce, where it had been set by the gov-
ernments of major countries, to about $60 and Mary's father's
coins jumped in value.

When I suggested to Mary she use gold bullion coins for part
of her inflation protection, she loved the idea. She knew from
her father just how solid a hedge gold could be. In this regard,
Mary is a bit different from many folks. Most people believe
bank accounts and stocks and bonds are the investments of
quality. Gold, to them, seems slightly offbeat.

It isn't, and history proves it. Unique among investments,
it has minimal practical uses yet is universally valued.

Like real estate, gold is available in a variety of ways. Bullion—
as gold bars or ingots—is one. The problem here is twofold: Bullion is both relatively illiquid and a problem to store.

Gold bullion coins are another investment vehicle. South
African Kruggerands, Canadian Maple Leafs, American Eagles
and Chinese Pandas have ready markets and an easily calculated
value, explaining why many investors find them an excellent vehicle for inflation protection.

Consider gold stocks. These are the stocks of companies exclusively or principally in the gold mining business. Gold stocks
are particularly worthwhile because they provide exceptional
leverage potential. Gold stocks can be quite volatile, which is
what you want for inflation protection. If a mining company

breaks even when gold sells for $400 an ounce and gold is selling for $405 per ounce, the company's profits are $5 per ounce. But, if gold's price moves up 2 percent to $415, the mining company's profits per ounce go to $15, that's a 200-percent increase. The reverse is also true, which is why gold mining companies' stock prices often swing like monkeys on a tree limb.

My usual recommendation to clients is not to buy gold stocks individually but, as with common stocks in general, to buy mutual funds that hold gold stocks. This way you get diversification, liquidity, lower risk (because the fund spreads its investments among a number of gold companies) and professional management.

In sum, as an inflation hedge, gold is a good performer that deserves serious consideration. In fact, it is an even better hedge against the unthinkable, such as a nuclear 9/11, which many of our leaders agree is likely, not just possible, but likely. The heads of the 9/11 Commission were on "Meet the Press," and when asked, all agreed that it is "probable" we will have a nuclear event in the United States.

THE DOWNSIDE

Every investment with an upside (profit potential) has a downside (loss potential). Investments used for inflation protection will likely do poorly in a depression and give a mediocre return in a period of relative price stability. During the time of high inflation in the late 1970s, gold rocketed in price to as high of $850 per ounce. Starting in the early 1980s and continuing through the early 2000s, gold generally traded from $350 to $450 per ounce with little movement above this and there was a period (roughly 1998 to 2001) when it dipped below $300 per ounce.

This lack of volatility hasn't made gold a particularly good investment over the past quarter century, which is what you would expect, since it's an inflation hedge and inflation hasn't been strong during that period. Remember, we don't expect inflation-protection investments to sparkle during periods of very moderate inflation. The idea is to design your portfolio so that if a particular economic situation develops, you'll have investments that take advantage of it, while others will do adequately or poorly. It doesn't matter what happens economically as long as the portfolio can handle all possibilities. This is what Bulletproofing your portfolio is all about, and is why we now use gold stock mutual funds in all our clients' portfolios—we get more bounce for the invested dollar, and at low risk.

YOUR PORTFOLIO

For all levels of risk, I recommend the portfolios on the protection side be pretty much the same. You should devote about 15 percent of your total assets to inflation protection. If you have $500,000 in investment assets, not including your home, about $75,000 should be in inflation protection investments. The 15 percent that is dedicated to inflation protection comprises 5 percent that goes into a gold-stock mutual fund and 10 percent that goes into real estate.

Low-risk portfolio: Two investments for you: real estate, 10 percent of your total assets—fully paid real estate, not leveraged real estate bought with something down and the rest borrowed; and gold-stock mutual funds (5 percent of your total assets).

Medium-risk portfolio: As a middle-of-the-road risk taker, put 15 percent of your total portfolio in inflation protection. You need less than the low-risk investor because you are willing to take on a bit more risk and be a bit more aggressive with your investments. Two investments are for you: A gold-stock mutual fund (5 percent of your total portfolio) and real estate (10 percent of your total portfolio and, unlike the low-risk investor, you can use leverage up to 50 percent with your real estate).

High-risk portfolio: For those really willing to take a flier, 5 percent of the total portfolio in a gold-stock mutual fund and 10 percent of the total portfolio needs to be in real estate. Your primary inflation-protection investment will be highly leveraged real estate, meaning you borrow 80 percent or more of the purchase price.

Are you starting to see a pattern? The reason that the protection investments have the same percentage in all portfolios is because everyone needs the protection to make sure that if a recession or depression, a nuclear 9/11, or any other crisis occurs that would destroy the market everyone can get their money back. No matter if you are a low-risk person or a high-risk person, everyone I know would like to have their money back so they can start over.

THE TERRORISTS
OF WALL STREET

BIG IS BAD

>   If you want to know why your returns have been so
> lousy . . .
>   If you need to know how to evaluate a brokerage firm
> or a financial planning firm . . .
>   If you want to make sure you get good help for a
> change . . .
>   **You need to read this chapter.**

I'm wondering how to be polite about the topic I'm addressing in this chapter. I'm having trouble. I can't be even-handed. I can't be dispassionate. I can't be totally objective, either. That's because the topic of this chapter is big brokerage firms and many of the other large and best-known financial institutions, and how they have been mistreating individual investors for decades.

Scandals have followed these companies around like puppies follow their owners: No matter what you do, they just keep coming back and doing it over and over again. I'm going to show in a moment just how bad the behavior of Wall Street is toward its average investors.

But before I do, let me say that the subject of this chapter isn't about how bad the major stock brokerage firms, insurance companies and even mutual fund companies can be. The subject of this chapter is, *Why you should not use big brokerage firms and other big financial institutions to manage your finances; instead, use the services of a competent, independent financial advisor.*

> Full disclosure: I am a competent, independent financial planner, so my extolling the virtues of people like me certainly has an element of self-justification. I'm coming right out and admitting that to you.

I am talking about those independent financial planners who have years of experience, who know what they're doing, who have long track records of success when investing their clients' money and who are honest and forthright.

Sure, I like to think of myself as a member of this group, but there are hundreds of others like me. If you hire any of them, I gain absolutely nothing and that's fine with me. I'm not trying to tell you how wonderful I am. I am telling you the big Wall Street firms are terrible for you and the small, independent planner who knows what he or she is doing, can be your best financial friend. Someone like that can make the difference between your having a financially secure retirement and your having to work far longer than you wanted or perhaps being scared every time you look at your monthly statement from your brokerage firm.

When you choose between the big boys and the independents, you choose between:

- Security and predictability versus insecurity, uncertainty and unpredictability.
- Good financial returns versus mediocre (or worse) financial returns.
- Honesty versus dishonesty.
- Effectiveness versus incompetence.
- Openness versus secrecy.
- A good result versus a lousy result.

WHY ARE THE BIG BROKERAGE FIRMS SO BAD?

The bottom line about big brokerage firms: It is more profitable for them to take advantage of the investor than for them to do right by the investor. They develop money-devising ways of getting around government and industry rules and regulations to take investors to the cleaners. I am saying this unequivocally. What I am saying is not an exaggeration. And I'll go into great detail about the scandals that the major Wall Street firms have brought down upon themselves.

Studies have been published showing that 75 percent of the profits of big brokerage firms come from their investment banking services. I had a New York Stock Exchange executive on my radio show make the comment that all the big brokerage firms are about the same because their people are like lemmings—they flow from one firm to the other. Even if you have a hundred million dollars invested with a big brokerage firm, that isn't significant to them because they may make 1 or 2 percent a year just investing your money. This is nothing to them. If they are regularly doing business with certain hedge funds, they probably help sell the hedge fund on which they make a bunch of money in syndicating it. They also get the loan for them and make hundreds of millions there, they then refinance it making hundreds of millions again, they then make an additional stock offering making, and you guessed it, hundreds of millions more.

You can see why even a client with a hundred million dollars may not be substantial to them. They often take advantage of investors by putting them in the funds they sell that make them the most money. Usually, the investments they sell are the worst type, such as hedge funds. Hedge funds have experienced a failure rate of as much as 20 percent in one year. This isn't exactly what I would call a good place to put your money and oftentimes hedge funds, despite their incredible risk, have under performed the market itself.

And, oh yes, in my opinion the big brokerage firms rob and steal from the investor because they can get away with it. The fines and penalties the SEC and other government agencies impose are so puny, so inconsequential, and so insignificant, that these firms have no incentive whatsoever to stop their behavior. In fact, they suffer so little for all their behavior that they have *positive incentives* to shaft the investor even more. Major drug dealers keep doing what they're doing because they usually suffer lightly at the hands of the law, yet reap enormous rewards from their illegal activities. Politicians can promise or say whatever they want because no one holds them accountable. And big financial institutions stick it to the investor because, well, they can. No one stops them. No one punishes them in any serious way. No one gives them any real incentives to do the right thing. Instead, they have plenty of incentives to do wrong by the individual investor because doing wrong means they make a lot of money.

The Really Stupid: Thinking you will get Bulletproofing from the Big Boys.

You will never, EVER see a big brokerage firm offer you a Bulletproofing strategy. Why? For one thing, the broker you deal with, who may call himself or herself a "financial planner" is, in fact, a stockbroker. What is a stockbroker? A sales person. Period. He or she is not a financial planner, no matter what they or their employer calls them. Don't believe me? Ask them what kind of training they've received. You will find that all the brokers of the major brokerage firms are trained, first and foremost, in selling. SELLING, NOT FINANCIAL PLANNING.

They are salespeople. And you should never forget that. There are good people who work at the big brokerage firms.

The problem is that they work in a very caustic environment that demands they do bad things like churn accounts, boost commissions and forget what is right for the clients. In an environment like this, it is difficult for anyone to maintain his or her integrity.

Big brokers don't do Bulletproofing because they're about selling, not about doing what's right for the client. These firms are nothing but glorified "boiler rooms," places where people cold-call prospects and hope and pray that one out of a hundred will be gullible enough to say, "Yes, take my money and invest it for me." If you've fallen into that trap, you are not alone. Millions of individual investors have signed up with the big boys only to regret it later. Don't take my word for it. This is a quote from a March 27, 2005 article in *The Miami Herald*:

> The FINRA announced it fined Citigroup Global Markets [part of Citibank, the world's largest bank], American Express Financial Advisors [part of American Express, the major financial services company] and Chase Investment Services [part of J.P. Morgan Chase, the country's second largest bank] $21.25 million for improper mutual fund sales practices that began in 2002. FINRA figures more than 50,000 investors were harmed.

Yes, you read that correctly: more than 50,000 investors were harmed from this one case.

Now let's do a little arithmetic. These three financial companies, which are three of the largest, most revered and best known in the world, were fined $21,250,000. They took to the cleaners *"more than"* 50,000. Let's say it was 50,000, period. How much were they fined? Do the math.

It comes out to $425 apiece.

They started these illegal practices in 2002 and were fined in 2005, so they probably did them for two years or more. That works out to $212.50 a year. I don't know how much they cost each of their 50,000 or more clients, but my guess is it was a lot more than $212.50 per year. That's chump change and our government, in its infinite wisdom, gently slapped them on the wrist and said, "No, bad dog, bad dog," just like you do with a puppy you are fond of. You don't really punish the puppy and the government doesn't really punish Wall Street.

THE WALL STREET-WASHINGTON CONNECTION

Ever wonder why Wall Street is able to get away with so much, all the while with the government looking at it? How can the big Wall Street firms take advantage of investors—over and over and over again—and get away with it while paying so little?

The answer is quite simple. Here's how the Wall Street-Washington connection works. Bright, ambitious men and women start their careers with a government agency, such as the Securities and Exchange Commission or comparable state agency, or an industry association, such as the Financial Industry Regulatory Authority. They work hard and learn the ropes—how the industry works, how the government and industry oversee brokerage firms, how high finance operates, how the relationship between the public and private sectors work. They become very knowledgeable and savvy about Wall Street and the people overseeing it.

Then, once they have all this knowledge and insight, what do they do? They jump ship and go to the opposing side. Yes, the best and the brightest spend the remainder of their careers working for the big Wall Street brokerage firms' back offices, banks, mutual fund companies, the big insurance companies and the rest. Their payoff for going over to the Dark Side: Money, big money. Their old buddies are still working for the government. If something goes wrong, they work things out with their buddies. The government gets to say it fined Wall

Street and Wall Street gets to keep doing what it's been doing because the punishments are so slight, so insignificant.

It's a very buddy-buddy, cozy arrangement. Very nice for everyone involved except, of course, the individual investor who is left out in the cold.

WHERE THE PROFITS COME FROM: BIG FIRMS VERSUS INDIVIDUAL FINANCIAL PLANNERS

Why, you may wonder, do the big firms want so much to poorly serve the little guy? And, for that matter, why would individual financial planners be different? Why don't financial planners have the same incentives as the big brokers to poorly serve the small investor?

The numbers tell the story: For the big firms, much of their profits come from big clients, such as corporations who do financing business with them or heavyweight investors with millions of dollars to invest. The investor contributes little to the big firms' bottom line. Of the billions of dollars the big Wall Street houses earn each year, pennies on the dollars come from smaller investors. These are investors with $20 million or less in assets. Sure, for most people, $10 million or $20 million is an unfathomable amount of money, but on Wall Street, people with this kind of money—and a lot more—are fairly commonplace. They want the people with the really big bucks, not just big bucks. The Wall Street firms, by giving their best service to their best customers are, in fact, serving their customer base well. Only their real customer base isn't investors but is, in fact, large investors and corporations.

Now look at the independent financial planners. They also serve their real customer base well. Who is that base? It's the individual investor. *One hundred percent of the profits of independent financial planners come from individual investors.*

Both groups—the big brokerage firms and the independent financial planners—do a very good job of serving their most important customers. The difference is, the most important customers of both groups come from very different economic strata. If you are super wealthy or head a major corporation, then by all means, use the services of the major Wall Street firms. But if you are an investor with less than one hundred million dollars, watch out for Wall Street. You just don't bring in enough profit for Wall Street to want to do right by you. It is better off taking advantage of you and making money from you that way.

HOW IT WORKS

How the big firms take advantage of investors is no secret. There are a number of techniques, and while I won't go into all of them here, a couple are worth noting.

One way is when they tout the stocks of the companies that are their clients. The companies may be selling their stock and, what do you know? the brokerage firm's tell their customers this stock is a great buy. This happened over and over during the boom years of the 1990s, and it's a practice that happens less now, but probably still happens in one form or another, and will happen again when enough time has passed.

Remember, the men and women working on Wall Street are very smart. If one way to take advantage of the public has been blocked, chances are they will find a new one. Most of the people who worked on Wall Street during these scandals, are still working there. If you think they have changed their stripes, I have a bridge in Brooklyn I would like to sell you.

The Really Stupid: Buying the recommendations of the big brokerage firms.

The media is part of this, too. The number of articles or broadcast programs saying how wonderful this stock or that is, or this investment strategy or that, or this brokerage firm or that, is uncountable. The media are filled with information about investing and Wall Street and corporate America—and much of it is wrong, just plain wrong. The people writing the articles are not financial planners and know nothing about the topic, so they have to rely on "experts." Who are these experts? What do you know; they are people from the big Wall Street in-stitutions. These institutions feed the media a line of junk, and the media, which doesn't know any better, just repeats it.

The Really Stupid: Thinking that the various periodicals are writing knowledgeable articles.

If you think I'm exaggerating, just look at articles from such "respected" publications as *Forbes, Fortune, The Wall Street Journal, Money, Business Week* and others from the late 1990s. See what they wrote about tech stocks, the market and its "inevitable" rise, the wonderfulness of investing in Wall Street. Then look at the truth that has come out since then: the scandals involving the biggest brokerage firms, the biggest mutual fund companies and the biggest insurance companies. The list is endless. These were the very same companies the media was telling you were smart, savvy, upfront and honest. It has since come out that they were anything but.

Plus, check out the advertising in such publications. I once compared the companies cited in *Money* with the advertising in that magazine and, what a surprise, there was a direct correla-tion of who was written about and who advertised. The compa-nies held up as smart and savvy and well serving are, in fact, the very same companies that advertise in many publications.

The Really Stupid: The most serious accusations, the most serious problems, the most serious frauds were of the big brokerage firms. They committed so much fraud that there are some estimates that the big brokerage firms earned as much as a trillion dollars by recommending stocks they knew were bad. This has been by far the biggest fraud ever committed on the public in history and no one went to jail for it.

I could go on and on with tales about the travesties and wrongdoings of Wall Street. I could fill this entire book with stories about what Wall Street has done to investors, investigations taken against Wall Street and fines it has had to pay. But I don't want to bore you. The following is just a very minor slice of the entire story, but it is enough, I think, to give you a good idea of who is involved (virtually every big Wall Street firm), what they have done (many different things), the legal charges that have been brought against Wall Street (there are many) and the fines that have been levied (in the billions of dollars).

Don't take a chance that you will find an honest stockbroker at a major Wall Street firm. Stick to the independent financial advisor who has your best interest at heart—because he or she depends entirely on *you* for his or her living.

THE PROOF

I've been hard on Wall Street and with good reason, as I'll show you now. You may be interested to know that Merrill Lynch threatened to sue me. I read their threat letter on the air, ridiculed them, dared them to sue me and told them if they wanted to sue me, all they had to do was call me and make an appointment to accept service. I would then spend the rest of my life telling the world how Merrill Lynch operates. This is partly why they are my poster boys for the bad guys of the brokerage industry. The following is just a partial list of headlines related to the wrong doings that Merrill Lynch is accused of and, in my opinion, probably did, in fact, commit.

26 April 2002 Merrill Admits to Wrong Kind of Bull CBS News.com Analysts touting stock while within firm's emails calling it a 'piece of junk.'

30 July 2002 Senator Says Merrill Lynch Helped Enron 'Cook Books' *The New York Times* A Senate panel argued Merrill Lynch assisted in creating false revenue for Enron using compromised business practices.

19 September 2002 Merrill Covers Its Eyes, Fires Enron Bankers Forbes.com Fired executives who refused to testify in Enron-related investigations.

10 October 2002 Mighty Merrill Lynch Bogs Down in Legal Troubles *USA Today* Panel ruled in favor of a Pennsylvania couple and ordered Merrill Lynch to pay them $7.7 million for failing to advise them on how to protect the value of their stake in an internet company.

17 March 2003 SEC Charges Merrill Lynch, Four Merrill Lynch Executives with Aiding and Abetting Enron Accounting Fraud sec.gov Merrill Lynch and its former executives helped manipulate year-end transactions with Enron to help boost Enron's income and earnings.

28 April 2003 Joint Press Release sec.com The former managing director for Merrill Lynch is fined $4 million and permanently barred from the securities industry.

28 April 2003 Wall St. Deal is Finalized
CNNMoney.com Merrill Lynch and 9 other securities firms agreed to pay $1.4 billion after deceiving investors with corrupt stock market research set up to obtain investment banking fees.

15 October 2003 Former Enron Accountant, Merrill Lynch Executive Charged in Connection with Fraudulent 'Nigerian Barge' Deal usdoj.com Former vice president of Merrill Lynch charged in connection with the collapse of Enron.

21 April 2004 Merrill Lynch Ordered To Pay For Sexual Bias *The New York Times* Ordered to pay $2.2 million to one woman for discrimination

22 September 2004 Conspiracy With Merrill Lynch Charged in Enron Trial *The Associated Press* Conspired together on sham transactions.

9 March 2005 Merrill Fined $13.5 Million and Censured *The Associated Press* Fined for market timing of mutual funds.

14 March 2005 Delray Beach Woman Testifies Today Against Merrill Lynch *Boca Raton News* A former employee seeking $5 million for alleged sex discrimination.

9 May 2005 Fee-Based Accounts: A Poor Fit For Investors? businessweek.com Putting clients who traded infrequently into fee-based accounts.

18 August 2005 Repeat Offender, Merrill Lynch, Fined $10M cchwallstreet.com Fined by the New York Stock Exchange for an array of operational and supervisory problems.

19 December 2005 NASD Fines Merrill Lynch, Wells Fargo and Linsco $19.4 Million for Improper Sales of Class B

and C Mutual Fund Shares nasd.com Firms did not disclose to investors that an equal investment in Class A shares was available and in most cases was a better investment for them.

13 March 2006 Merrill Lynch Fined $2.5 Million over E-mails newyorkbusiness.com Failed to comply with SEC requests for e-mails.

15 March 2006 NASD Fines Merrill $5 Million in Settlement Over Improper Supervision Charges Registered Rep Small investors were referred to call centers that were not sufficiently supervised, leading to several improprieties.

19 April 2006 Insider Trading Scandal at Goldman and Merrill *The Journal of the Business Law Society* Employees charged with insider trading.

6 July 2006 Enron Reaches Settlement with Merrill Reuters Merrill agreed to pay $29.5 million in conjunction with their role in Enron's bankruptcy.

I don't want you to think that I have been unfair to Merrill Lynch. Here is just a taste of the scandals the rest of Wall Street has been involved with over the past few years, the fines it has paid and the comments knowledgeable observers have made. Here's my proof that everything I said is true and accurate.

The Miami Herald, 27 March 2005

Putnam was fined $40 million, the SEC said, because it wasn't upfront about the "Preferred Marketing Arrangements" it had with 80 broker-dealers from 2000 through 2003. Putnam paid the brokers to promote their funds by directing stock trades to those firms, the SEC said. That conveniently uses shareholders' money— the commissions on stock trades—to pay for marketing, which otherwise would have been the fund company's expense.

Earlier this month, Putnam finished another part of its settlement with the SEC over its scandal-plagued trading. It agreed to reimburse shareholders $153 million for market timing and excessive short-term trading in its funds.

Testimony to Congress by Rosemary Shockman, president of Public Investors Arbitration Bar Association as reported in Congressional Quarterly, March 2005

The [mutual fund] industry had common, institutionalized practices of undisclosed fees, which motivated the brokers to sell certain types of mutual funds to customers, whether they were in the best interests of the customer or not.

Newsday, 23 February 2005

Quick & Reilly Inc., the discount brokerage unit of Bank of America Corp., and Piper Jaffray Cos. agreed to pay $570,000 and $275,000, respectively, to settle charges that they operated "preferred partner programs" for a small number of mutual fund families. [This is favoring some mutual fund families over others in return for commissions.]

Seattle Times, February 2005

Bear Stearns, the nation's sixth-largest securities firm, violated federal laws intended to protect investors when it helped brokers make illegal after-hours mutual fund trades, the Securities and Exchange Commission (SEC) has concluded. . . .

The Baltimore Sun, 13 February 2005

If you ever commit a crime and are facing justice, you'd be wise to ask for punishment similar to what mutual fund companies get.

Throughout the mutual fund scandals of abusive trading practices and double-dealing to give favored customers privileges ordinary investors can't get, punishment almost always has boiled down to a fine and no admission of wrongdoing.

It goes something like this: "We didn't do it, and we won't do it again."

Wink, wink.

"Oh, and that enormous payment to settle? The regulators were overzealous in pursuing us."

AARP Study, December 2002

Nineteen percent of people in retirement had to go back to work due to their losses in the market, or are looking for work or may need to look for work because of their losses.

Why aren't the presidents of the major brokerage firms in jail? David Humphreville, head of the New York Stock Exchange Trader's Association says:

Because they move back and forth between the SEC and big brokerage firms and they are not going to put their members of the good old boys club in jail.

From *Money* magazine article entitled, "Scandals at a glance," as posted on CNN Money, 11 January 2004 [this is just part of *Money's* list of firms charged with scandals]:

Alliance Capital: Alliance agrees to pay $250 million in fines and to cut management fees by 20 percent over five years in a settlement with New York's Attorney General Eliot Spitzer

Bank of America: "Spitzer says that BofA helped Canary [Capital] place late trades. He and the SEC have brought criminal and civil charges against [a] BofA broker . . ."

Charles Schwab: "The broker says that market timing occurred in its Excelsior Funds and late trading in its Mutual Fund Marketplace accounts. Schwab has fired two employees for deleting related e-mails."

Morgan Stanley: "In a settlement with the SEC over charges that its brokers put clients in high-commission funds, the firm has agreed to a $50 million fine. Morgan paid a $2 million fine for illegal broker incentives."

"Prudential: "The firm has fired a dozen workers; five have since been charged with fraud by the SEC for market timing."

From CNNMoney.com, 14 January 2004

Securities regulators . . . charged Waddell & Reed with improperly urging customers to switch variable annuity contracts, which generated $37 million in commissions and cost clients almost $10 million.

The National Association of Securities Dealers said the Overland Park, Kansas-based company's recommendations resulted in 6,700 new contracts and, according to its analysis, at least 1,400 customers were likely to lose money by making the switches.

Los Angeles Times, 20 December 2002

Government regulators are expected to announce today that they have reached a long-awaited settlement with major Wall Street brokerages that would require the firms to pay more than $1 billion to resolve investigations of biased research by stock analysts.

Milwaukee Journal Sentinel, 26 January 2005

The Strong name will disappear into a new Wells Fargo & Co. mutual fund brand as Wells merges the Strong Funds into its operations this year.

The blending of Strong's funds into those run by San Francisco-based Wells Fargo, set to occur in the second quarter, will erase the once-proud brand name of a firm tarnished in the mutual fund scandal of 2003 and 2004.

The Wall Street Journal, 19 September 2003

The title of an article says it all: 'Timing' at Mutual Funds Can Cost [investors] 2% a Year

Associated Press, 20 December 2004

California State Attorney General Bill Lockyer filed a securities-fraud lawsuit Monday against Edward D. Jones & Co., alleging the investment giant received $300 million in improper payments to push seven mutual funds to its clients.

The announcement came the same day that the Securities and Exchange Commission settled with the St. Louis-based brokerage firm for $75 million, but Lockyer said clients who were deceived deserved a larger payout.

And let's not forget that these series of scandals began after it was revealed the very investments the big brokerage firms were touting to their customers were the same investments they were bad-mouthing to others.

CONTINUING TO WORK WITH LARGE BROKERAGE FIRMS

If, for some reason, you want to do this, one of the things you can do is to have your securities certificated. That is, if you have individual stocks and bonds, have them send out the certificates to you. That way, you actually hold the actual stocks and bonds, not the brokerage firm. If they then go under, you don't have to go through a long wait to get access to your investments again. Buy mutual funds through one of the large brokerage firms I recommend that own mutual funds directly through the company, such as American Funds or Franklin Templeton. That way, if the brokerage firm fails, it will not cause you any delays in accessing your mutual funds.

THINGS YOU CAN DO TO PROTECT YOURSELF

Stay away from these firms. One of the things you could do is simply move your investments out of the large brokerage firms that have investment banking functions. That includes Merrill Lynch, Smith Barney, Morgan Stanley, Prudential Securities, etc. Plus, you might want to consider why you would want to stay with a firm that has a history of giving you self-serving recommendations that could cost you money.

The Really Stupid: Doing business with Charles Schwab.

Avoid Charles Schwab. They have fees hidden in their mutual funds. They charge mutual funds up to 35 basis points at the time of this writing to be a part of their program. This causes the mutual funds to raise their charges and ends up costing you money, but it is sure a slick way of hiding the cost from you. Sure, it is in their disclosure information, but who actually *reads* that nonsense.

The Really Stupid: Buying mutual funds from the big brokerage firms.

One of the things we have seen a lot of in the mutual fund industry is companies taking their bad mutual funds and rolling them into their good mutual funds so that the track record of the bad fund disappears. If you look at the long-term track record of a mutual fund family, they usually only include the most recent funds that are available and they don't count the horrible performance of the funds that have been rolled into some of the better performing funds. Remember, numbers don't lie, but those manipulating the numbers do.

Don't buy mutual funds that are issued by the brokerage you are working with. Whether it's IDS, Merrill Lynch, Smith Barney, etc., because historically these mutual funds tend to be non-performers and they could represent an additional significant conflict of interest.

Work only with financial professionals. Most brokers have little or no credentials to be doing what they are doing and the results show in their performance. As a bare minimum, your advisor should have a business degree, hopefully a master's degree or the equivalent. Any financial advisor that you use should be a Registered Investment Advisor. Registered Investment Advisors are required by law to do what they believe to be in your best interests.

In addition, your advisor should have a Certified Financial Planner designation or the equivalent in training or experience so that you know they have the basics to provide you with paramount recommendations for your financial well being. I went through rigorous hours of studying to get my CFP designation, but recently decided to drop it because the CFP board became a tool of the bad guys. Every time one of the big firms would threaten to sue me, as Merrill Lynch did, someone in their firm filed a complaint against me with the Board of Standards and Practices of the Financial Planning Association.

This forced me to spend a tremendous amount of time and lawyer fees fighting false allegations. In addition, they would never tell me who was filing the complaint against me. Every other professional association I know of always gives you this information so that you can face your accusers. Of course, every single complaint that was filed against me was dismissed because they were ridiculous. When I do a radio show, I have the facts and I make it clear when something is my opinion. Last time I checked, freedom of speech is a right of every citizen of the United States.

In my firm, we have an intensive training program. It is my radio show. The preparation for my weekly show often takes 20 to 30 hours of my time per week, including tremendous amount of research on the behalf of all of the people who work for me. This is the most intensive training of any firm that I know of and all of the topics we research for our radio show benefits our clients.

Find someone who has the training to address all the important financial issues for you, such as estate planning. Estate planning is important to assure that your kids get your money and not the IRS or the attorneys when you die. A top-flight financial advisor should review your tax return before you become a client and every year thereafter.

A good financial professional will make sure you have the proper homeowner's, auto, life, disability, and health insurance, as well as making sure you're protected from identity theft. And last, but not least, such a professional assures your investments are proper for your situation.

IDENTITY THEFT

PROTECT YOURSELF FROM THE THEFT OF YOUR MOST VALUED ASSET . . . YOUR NAME

If you have credit cards, bank accounts, telephone numbers . . .

If you don't want to spend hundreds of hours straightening out purchases from retailers claiming you made purchases, which you did not . . .

If you don't like the idea of strangers having access to some of your most personal information . . .

You need to read this chapter.

When we think of theft, we usually think of something tangible, physical being stolen—a stereo, car, purse, cash. Today, there's a different kind of theft, very cutting edge, very up-to-date, that really wasn't a problem until the past few years. Now, it is very popular, and involves something that you cannot hold in your hand or carry or look at. It is one's identity.

It happened to one of my clients. Big time. I won't go into the details, but here's the bottom line: It took him two years, 500 hours of work and a fair amount of money to clear things up. Identity theft is like a major disease. It's something you don't think will ever happen to you, and chances are it won't, but if it does, it can become a major distraction and can throw your life into disarray.

The Bad: Thinking that identity theft is someone else's problem while it could become your problem.

83

A CRIME OF MAJOR PROPORTIONS

A Bulletin published by the U.S. Department of Justice notes: "Identity theft has been referred to by some as the crime of the new millennium. It can be accomplished anonymously, easily, with a variety of means, and the impact upon the victim can be devastating." Don't ignore that last word: Devastating.

Experts have estimated that in the past year as many as 15 million people became the victims of identity theft. That means that 28.5 people became a victim of this new crime every minute, or a new victim every 2 seconds. It seems inevitable that we all may become victims unless we are diligent in doing everything possible to protect ourselves. Even then, we are not guaranteed the safety of our most personal information. This may prove to become the most common crime in America today.

Identity theft is serious business. A bi-national study done for the Attorney General of the United States and the Solicitor General of Canada found: "Identity theft is never committed for its own sake. Criminals engage in identity theft because the acquisition of other people's identifying data enables them to engage in a growing variety of other criminal acts, such as fraud, organized crime, and terrorism."

The problem is so severe you could even end up in jail, as did a young lady who reported to work as an Assistant District Attorney. She was immediately arrested because someone had stolen her identity some months before and committed numerous crimes in her name. In the end, she was cleared of all charges, but spent several days in jail before it was straightened out.

Identity theft is the largest category of consumer fraud. It remains the #1 concern among consumers contacting the Federal Trade Commission.

Victims of identity theft face an enormous and arduous task in repairing both their credit rating and their emotional well being. One of the biggest obstacles they face is that they are, more or less, completely on their own in clearing their financial records. Law enforcement generally isn't equipped nor interested in helping victims of identity theft.

The prevailing attitude on the part of most creditors who are advised of an occurrence of identity fraud is one of downright skepticism. In fact, it's not uncommon for creditors to demand that identity-theft victims submit an affidavit testifying to the fact that they did not incur the debt themselves. There is actually a widely used affidavit form from the FTC. For a copy of it and instructions about how to deal with identity theft from the FTC, go to http://www.ftc.gov/bcp/conline/pubs/credit/affidavit.pdf. Adding insult to injury, creditors may require the submission of copies of the victim's driver's license, Social Security card, or birth certificate—this from folks whose identities were just stolen often via the same documentation.

Understandably, many victims in the midst of the quagmire of identity theft are not eager to hand over these personal identification items, particularly since many victims suspect that it is a creditor's negligence (i.e., such as requiring an inadequate verification of the identity of an applicant) that may have led to the identity theft in the first place. This is a crime that pits victims not just against perpetrators but also law enforcement and businesses. It's easy to see how frustrating, expensive and time consuming it can be to clear one's name when so many forces may be working against the victim.

Another unusual aspect of identity theft: It is a crime that victims don't often realize has happened until long after it begins. Almost all other crimes are known when they happen or shortly thereafter. It can sometimes take from one to six months before the crime is discovered. That's a long time for any crime.

WHAT IS IDENTITY THEFT?

When identity theft happens, you'll still be you, but someone else will be masquerading as you, as well.

"Identity theft occurs when someone uses your personal information such as your name, Social Security number, credit card number or other identifying information, without your permission to commit fraud or other crimes."

The U.S. Federal Trade Commission

"Identity theft and identity fraud are terms used to refer to all types of crime in which someone wrongfully obtains and uses another person's personal data in some way that involves fraud or deception, typically for economic gain."

The U.S. Department of Justice

"Identity theft is the fraudulent use of an individual's personal identifying information, such as a Social Security number, mother's maiden name, date of birth or bank account number."

Federal Bureau of Investigation

Is this something to worry about, or is it one of those crimes that, well, are far more likely to happen to someone other than you?

Consider that (as reported in *Consumer Reports*) identity theft:

- Claimed 33 million Americans since 1990 (about 1 in six adults)
- Costs victims around $800–$2000 apiece and requires about two years before their names are cleared
- Is committed against people of all races, incomes and ages
- Can even land you in jail because of other people committing fraudulent acts using your identification

According the Federal Trade Commission, the 10 states with the highest rates of identity theft in the country, in proportion to their population, are:

1. Illinois
2. California

3. Georgia

4. Arizona

5. Texas

6. Florida

7. New York

8. Pennsylvania

9. Colorado

10. Nevada

WAYS TO HAVE YOUR IDENTITY STOLEN

How can someone steal your identity, you are probably wondering. There are a number of ways:

- "Shoulder surfing," a term which according to the U.S. Department of Justice (DOJ) is when someone watches you (as in, over-your-shoulder) as you punch in your telephone calling card number or credit card number, or listens in on a conversation you are having where you give your credit card number or other valuable information to a hotel or rental-car-company clerk or the like.

- "Dumpster diving," which is another DOJ term and refers to someone who goes through the garbage of a communal dumpster to get copies of your checks, bank or credit card statements or other records that have sensitive information. Such information could include your name, address, telephone number, Social Security number and more.

- Direct mail. Ever get a "preapproved" credit card or credit card application, and throw it away without even opening it and certainly without cutting it up? Criminals have been known to retrieve such direct mail solicitations and have the cards activated for their own use without you being the wiser.

- Redirected mail. If criminals have access to your mail because it is in a common area, they can have it redirected elsewhere for their own use.

- The Internet. The Internet has become an important source of information about individuals that can be used for identity theft. Social Security numbers, telephone numbers, addresses, birth dates, employers and other personal information are readily available on the Internet for those who know where to look. A couple of examples illustrate just how vulnerable we all can be. In one federal prosecution, the defendants allegedly obtained the names and Social Security numbers of U.S. military officers from a website, then used more than 100 of those names and numbers to apply via the Internet for credit cards with a Delaware bank. In another federal prosecution, the defendant allegedly obtained personal data from a federal agency's website, then used the personal data to submit 14 car loan applications online to a Florida bank.

- Imposters. Sometimes the thief pretends to be you in order to gain access to valuable personal information about you. They may obtain your credit report, for example, by posing as a landlord, employer or someone else who may have a legitimate need for, and legal right to, the information.

- E-mail and website "Spoofing." According to the DOJ, many criminals who want to obtain personal data from people online use a technique known as "spoofing": the creation of e-mails and websites that appear to belong to legitimate businesses, such as financial institutions or online auction sites. Consumers who receive e-mails claiming to be from a legitimate business are often directed to a website, appearing to be from that business, at which the consumers are directed to enter large amounts of personal data. In fact, the criminals who created these e-mails and websites have no real connection with those businesses. Their sole purpose is to obtain the consumers' personal data to engage in various fraud schemes.

- Theft from company or government databases. In addition, according to the DOJ, law enforcement agencies in both Canada and the United States have noticed a significant increase in efforts by identity thieves to access large databases of personal information that private companies and government agencies maintain. Criminals have broken into offices to steal computer hard drives, bribed or compromised employees into obtaining personal data for them, and hacked into databases.

   In fact, a single thief *cum* hacker can steal millions of identities when they gain access to company databases or commercial websites where credit card information and other personal data are stored. These databases are becoming more and more common, in part because both businesses and governments are sharing everything from marketing lists to property records on the Internet. Even well-intentioned legislation is fueling the identity-theft problem. According to *Consumer Reports,* "The federal Gramm-Leach-Bliley Act of 1999, which allows financial institutions to share customer data with affiliated companies, opened the floodgates to the exchange of financial information, some privacy experts say."

- Your old computer. A study found that on one-third to one-half of old computers tested, MIT graduate students were able to recover sensitive files from their hard drives.

According to the ID Theft Data Clearinghouse, the most common types of identity theft are:

- Using or opening a credit card account fraudulently.
- Opening telecommunications or utility accounts fraudulently.
- Passing bad checks or opening a new bank account.
- Getting loans in another person's name.
- Working under another person's name.

HOW IDENTITY THIEVES USE YOUR PERSONAL INFORMATION

The ways thieves can make use of the identity information they steal from you is varied—and a bit frightening, given how wide ranging these ways are. Here are some examples cited by the DOJ:

- Thieves call your credit card issuers and, pretending to be you, ask to change the mailing address on your credit card account. The imposter then runs up charges on your account. Because your bills are being sent to the new address, it may take some time before you realize there is a problem.
- They open a new credit card account using your name, birth date and Social Security number. When they use the credit card and don't pay the bills, the delinquent account is reported on your credit report.
- They establish phone or wireless service in your name.
- They open a bank account in your name and write bad checks on that account.

- They file for bankruptcy under your name to avoid paying debts they've incurred under your name, or to avoid eviction.
- They counterfeit checks or debit cards and drain your bank account.
- They buy cars by taking out auto loans in your name.
- They give your name to the police during an arrest. If they're released from police custody but don't show up for their court date, an arrest warrant is issued in your name.

WHAT YOU CAN DO

The cheapest way to protect your identity (but not the best) is to order a copy of your credit report from each of the three major credit bureaus. Get copies of these reports at least once a year. These individual reports contain information on your address, your employment, credit accounts that have been opened in your name, your history of paying your bills, and whether you have been sued, arrested or filed for bankruptcy.

The Fair Credit Reporting Act (FCRA) requires each of the nationwide consumer reporting companies—Equifax, Experian, and TransUnion—to provide you with a free copy of your credit report, at your request, once every 12 months. The three nationwide consumer reporting companies have set up a central website, a toll-free telephone number, and a mailing address through which you can order your free annual report.

To order your credit reports, visit annualcreditreport.com, call 1-877-322-8228, or complete the Annual Credit Report Request Form and mail it to: Annual Credit Report Request Service, P.O. Box 105281, Atlanta, GA 30348-5281, or you can print it from ftc.gov/bcp/conline/edcams/credit. Do not contact the three nationwide consumer reporting companies individually. They are providing free annual credit reports only through annualcreditreport.com.

Check your credit reports carefully. Make sure the information is accurate. Be sure your name, address, Social Security number and employer are correct. Look for inquiries you didn't initiate, accounts you didn't open and unexplained debts on your legitimate accounts. Not all inaccuracies are nefarious; some are a result of typographical or other honest errors. If you do find an error whether due to fraud or mistake, notify the credit bureau immediately, *both* by phone and in writing. I'll address the issue of correcting errors and fraud shortly.

The Good: Signing up for a credit reporting service through one of the three major credit bureaus.

This can be done at www.equifax.com, www.experian.com or www.transunion.com. These services will include multiple credit reports per year, as well as daily updates to your credit. Many of them will also update your credit every night and let you know of any changes that have occurred during the past 24 hours. So, if any of the basic information changes such as your address, phone number, new account applications, or new credit cards, they will inform you by e-mail the following day. If you find that there is an application submitted for an American Express card, for instance, and you had not applied personally, you can have them put a watch on your credit and notify all three credit agencies. If they put a watch on your report, they will not verify any new credit applications unless they check with you first to make sure they are valid.

Keep in mind that inquiries on credit reports from potential credit card issuers or others do not always mean someone has tried to get credit in your name. Banks and credit card companies often inquire about a consumer's creditworthiness to help them target their marketing efforts. These inquiries will be identified in a designated section of the report.

In addition to getting copies of your credit reports, adopt a "need to know" approach to your personal data. A credit card company may need to know your mother's maiden name so it can verify your identity when you call to inquire about your account. However, a person who calls you and says he or she is from your bank, doesn't need to know that information if it is already on file with your bank. If someone calls you and says he or she is from your bank and needs to know your mom's maiden name, try to find out who they are and report them to the police.

Also, on a need-to-know basis, keep the information on your personal checks to a minimum. Some states require you have your address printed on your checks, others don't. If you don't have to put your address on your check, why do so? Don't have your phone or Social Security number printed on your checks, either. The more information you have on your checks, the more information you are routinely handing out to strangers, who don't need it and who may decide to use it in ways harmful to you.

Solicitation calls should also be viewed very skeptically. If someone calls and wants to know personal information—on the pretext of giving you a credit card, a prize or something else of value—ask them to send an application by regular mail. If they refuse, say you're not interested and hang up. If they send the application, check it out carefully, call the Better Business Bureau, and be sure you're dealing with a reputable, legitimate company. Don't give out your Social Security number, credit card number or expiration date or other potentially valuable information over the phone without knowing who you are talking to and why they need the information.

When traveling, have your mail held at the post office or have a neighbor take it. Don't have it pile up where it can be taken and used by thieves.

If you have bank accounts or credit cards, be sure you receive monthly statements. Check to see that these statements are for the most recent month or reporting period and are not from some time ago.

Maintain careful records of your banking, credit card, stock brokerage and other financial accounts.

And, yes, lie. I went to a gym in Las Vegas that wanted my Social Security number. That's crazy. Why would a gym need my Social Security number? I wouldn't give it to them and they wouldn't let me into the gym. Then I got wise. The next time I went there, I gave them a phony Social Security number, something I made up on the spot and they let me in. If it's going to be less hassle to give them a phony Social Security number, then make one up. There's no legitimate reason I can think of that a store or service provider or gym needs my Social Security number. Of course, make sure your real number isn't on your driver's license, checks or any other place that can easily be looked at.

Note: It is against the law to use a phony Social Security number. But I checked with Utah's attorney general, who said if the purpose of using a phony Social Security number is to avoid people getting your number, he doubts that anybody would prosecute you for making a "mistake" on a couple of digits in your Social Security number. I'm not recommending that anyone break the law. Use your own judgment.

Remember, if you are victimized, in most instances as a consumer you are protected by law from fraudulent charges over $50. The problem is that you have to prove to very skeptical creditors that the charges are indeed fraudulent—someone other than you made them without your knowledge or consent. This can prove to be quite problematic.

WHO TO CONTACT

If you've been the victim of identity theft, think you might have been, or just want to monitor your credit to make sure you have not been, you need to contact the three principal credit reporting companies:

Equifax

1. To report fraud, call: 800-525-6285 or write to P.O. Box 740250, Atlanta, GA 30374-0250.

2. To order a copy of your credit report ($8 in most states), write to P.O. Box 740241, Atlanta, GA 30374-0241, or call 800-685-1111.

3. To dispute information in your report, call the phone number provided on your credit report.

4. To opt out of pre-approved offers of credit, call 888-567-8688, or write to Equifax Options, P.O. Box 740123, Atlanta, GA 30374-0123.

Experian (formerly TRW)

1. To report fraud, call 888-EXPERIAN or 888-397-3742, fax to 800-301-7196, or write to P.O. Box 1017, Allen, TX 75013.

2. To order a copy of your credit report ($8 in most states): P.O. Box 2104, Allen, TX 75013, or call 888-EXPERIAN.

3. To dispute information in your report, call the phone number provided on your credit report.

4. To opt out of pre-approved offers of credit and marketing lists, call 800-353-0809 or 888-5OPTOUT or write to: P.O. Box 919, Allen, TX 75013.

<u>TransUnion</u>

1. To report fraud, call 800-680-7289 or write to P.O. Box 6790, Fullerton, CA 92634.

2. To order a copy of your credit report ($8 in most states), write to P.O. Box 390, Springfield, PA 19064 or call 800-888-4213.

3. To dispute information on your report, call the phone number provided on your credit report.

4. To opt out of pre-approved offers of credit and marketing lists, call 800-680-7293 or 888-5OPTOUT or write to P.O. Box 97328, Jackson, MS 39238.

<u>Others</u>

There may be other organizations you need to call too, such as:

- Your long-distance telephone company if your long-distance calling card has been stolen or you find fraudulent charges on your bill.

- Banks and other financial institutions, if you've found your identity has been stolen or if accounts have been created in your name without your permission or knowledge. You may need to cancel accounts, change your personal identification number (PIN) used with your ATM card, and stop payment on checks that have not yet cleared.

Let the Federal Trade Commission know of your situation, by going to its website (www.ftc.gov), calling: 877-ID-THEFT (877-438-4338) or sending a written description to: Consumer Response Center, FTC, 600 Pennsylvania Avenue, N.W., Washington, DC 20580.

Other federal agencies that might become involved:

- Postal Inspection Service
- Social Security Administration
- Internal Revenue Service

PRIVACY

Privacy issues are related to identity theft and protection. Privacy is increasingly an issue for all of us, which is why I'm including a brief discussion of it here.

The federal government instituted a program that allowed you to place your phone number off limits to telemarketers. This "do not call" list was beefed up by having telemarketers face penalties of up to $11,000 per call made to those on the list and allowing consumers to sue for up to $500 per call if the telemarketing companies do not abide by the new regulation. Non-profit and political callers were exempt from the new regulation and businesses can call consumers up to 18 months following a sale.

When I first heard about this legislation, I was joyous. Those annoying calls in the evening would be completely eliminated or so I thought. But when I researched this bill, I found out it was a horrible piece of work. It prevents all calls from people who most of us would not consider telemarketers.

Any professionals that we work with are prevented from calling under this law. This includes your attorney, dentist and even your doctor, though they have our permission to call us. In fact, most of us want them to call. For example, if you have a trust and the attorney promises to call you when there are major changes to the law and there is a major change two years down the road, he can't call because that is telemarketing and it is beyond the 18-month deadline.

If you are out of town for a year and a half and you want your dentist to call when you get back to schedule a check-up, guess what, he can't call because that is telemarketing and he hasn't done business with you during the past 18 months.

This nonsense law lumps the good guys together with the bad guys and prevents everyone from calling, even those you want to hear from.

If these things seem to be a problem to you as they do to me, then what you can do is very straightforward:

- Put your telephone number on the not-published list. This way, it does not appear in the phone book, but people can get it from Information.
- Send out letters with every bill that you get saying that they are not to give out your public or private information to anyone and don't send solicitations. That limits the amount of not just sales calls you receive, but the amount of junk mail you receive as well.

The people I know who have implemented these simple strategies have drastically reduced the junk mail and the phone calls from solicitors that they receive at home to the point that they are almost nonexistent.

A RECAP

What you can do to protect yourself:

1. Protect your Social Security number. Don't give it out unless you absolutely have to. There are even laws that make it a federal crime to ask you for your Social Security number more than once if you have already refused

to give it out. So, be adamant about making sure that someone absolutely has to have your Social Security number before you give it out.

2. Shred everything with your name, Social Security number, birth date and family information that may give your mother's maiden name. Be especially careful to shred every one of those preapproved credit card applications and cards.

3. If your mail stops suddenly, be suspicious. Check with the Post Office immediately to make sure that a phony change of address has not been filed.

4. Sign up for a Credit Watch service through one of the three major credit bureaus.

CONSUMER QUIZ

The Criminal Division of the DOJ offers the following identity theft quiz for consumers:

Identity Theft: A Quiz for Consumers
Identity thieves use many ways of getting your personal financial information so they can make fraudulent charges or withdrawals from your accounts. Do you know how you can reduce the risk of becoming a victim of identity theft? Take this simple quiz, and see how you score:
Correct answers: *Yes* to all

1. When I keep my ATM cards and credit cards in my wallet, I never write my PIN (Personal Identification Number) on any of my cards.

   Reason: If you lose your ATM or credit card, identity thieves or other criminals can have instant access to your bank or credit card account.

2. When I leave my house, I take with me only the ATM and credit cards I need for personal or business purchases.

Reason: If your wallet or purse is lost or stolen, and you're carrying fewer cards, you'll have to make fewer calls to banks and credit card companies to report the losses, and the odds of fraudulent charges in your name will be lower.

3. When I get my monthly credit card bills, I always look carefully at the specific transactions charged to my account before I pay the bill.

Reason: Someone who gets your credit card number and expiration date doesn't need the actual card to charge purchases to your account. If you don't look closely at your credit card statement each month you might not have any recourse if fraudulent transactions go through and you don't dispute them promptly with your credit card company. As soon as you see unauthorized charges on your statement, contact the credit card company immediately to report them.

4. When I get my monthly bank statements, credit-card bills, or other documents with personal financial information on them, I always shred them before putting them in the trash.

Reason: Some identity thieves aren't shy about "dumpster diving"—literally climbing into dumpsters or rooting through trash bins to look for identifying information that someone threw out. Buying and using a shredder at your home or office is an inexpensive way to frustrate dumpster divers and protect your personal data.

5. When I get mail saying I've been pre-approved for a credit card, and don't want to accept or activate that card, I always tear up or shred the pre-approval forms before putting them in the trash.

Reason: If you throw out the documents without tearing them up or shredding them, dumpster divers" can send them back to the credit card company, pretending to be you and saying your address has changed. If they can use the account from a new location, you may not know the account's being used in your name until you see it on a credit report.

6. I request a copy of my credit report at least once a year.

Reason: Reviewing your credit report can help you find out if someone has opened unauthorized financial accounts, or taken out unauthorized loans, in your name. All consumers qualify for a free copy of their credit reports. Contact www.annualcreditreport.com.

7. If the volume of the mail I get at home has dropped off substantially, I always check with my local post office to see if anyone has improperly filed a change-of-address card in my name.

Reason: Some identity thieves may try to take over your credit card and bank accounts, and delay your discovery of their criminal activities, by having your mail diverted to a new address where they can go through it without your knowledge. Your local post office should have on file any change-of-address cards and can respond if you find that someone is improperly diverting your mail.

8. If I think that I may be a victim of identity theft, I immediately contact:

- The Federal Trade Commission to report the situation and get guidance on how to deal with it.

- The three major credit bureaus to inform them of the situation.

- My local police department to have an officer take a report.

- Any businesses where the identity thief fraudulently conducted transactions in my name.

Reason: Identity theft is a crime under federal law, and under the laws of most states, that carries serious penalties including imprisonment and fines. To help law enforcement in investigating and prosecuting identity theft, the Federal Trade Commission (FTC) maintains a national database of complaints by identity theft victims. The FTC, through a toll-free hotline (877-ID-THEFT), can also help you decide what steps to take in trying to remedy the situation and restore your good name and credit. Credit bureaus should also be notified so that they can flag your credit report. Local police, by taking a report and providing you with a copy, can help you show creditors that an identity thief has been conducting certain transactions in your name and without your permission.

RISK

It Doesn't Have to Be Risky

If you want to limit your risk while still getting great returns . . .

If you want to adhere to Bruce's First law and not lose the money . . .

If you want to make smart investments and avoid the really stupid ones . . .

You need to read this chapter.

You can plan and plan for retirement, but even the best-laid plans can run afoul of the unknown. For example, when creating a strategy for your financial future, you must make certain assumptions, such as the rate of return your investments are expected to earn and what the rate of inflation will be.

No one knows with certainty what the future holds. When you make assumptions about something, you run the risk that your assumptions will not come true.

There's a word in the above sentence that's particularly noteworthy—risk. Risk is with us always, whether we are driving down a street or investing our money. Not only do we continually face various types of risks but also our tolerance for risk varies from person to person. The types of risk we're willing to subject ourselves to vary between individuals as well.

Someone might be willing to risk their money playing poker or investing in a stock, but be deathly afraid of taking any physical risk, such as climbing a mountain or scuba diving. On the other hand, a mountain climber may love the adrenaline rush of taking a physical risk, but put all his or her money into government bonds because financial risks are too terrifying to deal with.

I ask every client, "How much risk are you willing to take?" When they say, "I'm a medium-risk person," (or whatever risk level they think they are), I have them rank themselves on a scale of 1 to 5. After protracted conversations with them, the vast majority of the time I find they know their risk level very well and it is an appropriate level for their age and station in life. Once in a while I will get someone who will come in and say, "I want no risk and 100 percent a year return," or "I want no risk and I want 12 percent a year." Either one of these is about the same thing because neither is possible. Normally, after some discussion, we come to a reasonable agreement about what their risk level really needs to be to achieve the return that they want.

My Bulletproofing strategy cuts most risk over the long term, but no strategy can completely eliminate risk, especially in the short-to-medium terms. Even if a strategy could, you wouldn't want it. That's because risk and reward are related. If there is no risk, then there is no return.

HOW I DO BULLETPROOFING

First, I help shield investments from things that can devastate them in the long term by using Treasury bonds, gold, real estate and other protection investments. Second, I use Modern Portfolio Theory to tell us how many baskets and how many eggs we need in each basket. This helps us choose the asset classes like treasury bonds, gold, international bonds, real estate foreign stocks, large-cap value stocks, all the different classes we might choose from. And then, finally, we go into each asset class and sometimes change the investments in that class depending on circumstances. An example is when I found that Korea had changed its banking laws that had contributed to the country being in a depression. I felt that it was a low-risk, smart move to take out the broad-based emerging-markets fund in that asset class and replace it with just Korea. This served us very well. From April of 2001 to the end of 2006, the Korea fund I used had a cumulative return of 353.25%; that's an annual average of 30.56%.

Many times, making these types of changes actually lowers the risk while increasing the potential return because we are normally buying investments with lower P/E ratios than the average in any given asset class.

This type of risk reduction with increased returns requires extensive research. I do such research every week not just because of my clients, but I'm forced to because of my weekly radio program. I have to have the most up to date information because I have tens of thousands of listeners who will know if I'm wrong or winging it. One of the principal reasons my investment choices have been so successful is because of the tremendous amount of time that all my staff and I spend researching investment alternatives and other areas that relate to our clients.

> **The Good: When you take a risk that is intelligently evaluated and you have done a good job of deciding what all the risks really are, then you can be sure rewards are worth the risks involved.**

Not all risk is obvious, not even when you are looking for it. Here's a piece of advice I once got from one of my business school professors: I told him I was reviewing an investment but that I couldn't see the risk in it, I couldn't find the "holes" in the story behind the investment. He sagely replied: "Well, Bruce, if you want to know where the risk is in that investment, buy it and you will find out." Every investment has a risk, and you should never forget that.

RISK

One important aspect of risk that is paramount, but often unacknowledged in making investment decisions, is its effect on your behavior. If you don't like risk, yet put money into commodities futures contracts (among the riskiest of investments), you'll probably react quickly to market fluctuations and endanger your investment, giving in to panic at the first wide swing in price and getting out when you should stay in. Or you freeze and do nothing. People don't think rationally or effectively when panicked and afraid, and that's not a good frame of mind to be in when making crucial decisions affecting your financial future.

A couple came into my office. The husband was 39 years old and they had just made about $1.5 million in a booming real estate market. It was now enough money that they were concerned about losing it. I explained to them, as I do with all my clients, "Give me the money you don't want to lose." And that's the money we Bulletproof. Some people want to have a play account where they buy and sell individual stocks or other things that grab their interest. Fine, but understand that that money is at great risk. I have no problem with people doing that as long as they have enough money protected by Bulletproofing. This is a way to protect yourself and still deal with your desire for considerable risk, assuming you want to take a lot of risk.

The Bad: The twin evils, fear and greed, are the bane of successful investing. Fear, when something goes down and you bail out because you've taken too much risk. Greed, when something is going up, you pile on more hoping to make a killing. The smart investor eliminates emotion from the decision-making process.

> **The Really Stupid: If you can't put your head on your pillow and fall asleep free of worry each night because your investments scare you to death, you're in the wrong investments.**

A woman of 80 once came to my office and before I could introduce myself asked, "What's the market doing today?" She was in trouble and scared silly about her financial situation and this made her chronically nervous.

Going broke wasn't her concern, for she had plenty of money. Instead, she fretted unhealthily about losing money. In short, her investments were too risky for her personality. She owned aggressive growth stocks that do well in the long term but, day by day, are as explosive as a 2-year-old's temper. Together, we changed her investments to match personality, dumping the high-risk stocks in favor of income-oriented mutual funds and secure—and calming—bonds. As her portfolio stopped its manic swings, she mellowed and eventually lost her nervous edge entirely.

Moderate-risk-takers are just as susceptible to investments with inappropriate risks. If they buy boring CDs, disappointment will follow. They like the excitement of bigger returns and the gambling aspect of taking risks obviously generates excitement. So they do something foolish, like buying the penny stock of a firm that's never sold a thing and is unlikely ever to do so. Or they go into commodities they know nothing about. Soon they're having more excitement than they ever wanted. I call this a recipe for disaster. Successful investing requires a match between risk and personality.

WHERE THERE'S REWARD, THERE'S USUALLY RISK

The more risk, the greater the potential reward or profit; the less risk, the smaller the likely reward. This trade-off is basic to all investing, with risk having an essential role in every investment decision you make. Having said that, it's worth noting that at certain times, it is possible, through the use of modern portfolio theory, to boost returns while at the same time reducing risk. But in general, getting more return usually involves taking on additional risk.

Risk affects you directly through price fluctuations. The prices of everything you buy can change at any given moment and, by their nature, these changes are short-to-medium term. That's how long they affect you. Yet you should hold for the long term so that your earnings reflect the long-term growth trends of your investments, leaving temporary worries about short-term fluctuations behind you.

One of my clients learned this the hard way. During the two years she held a gold mutual fund, its price dropped about 20 percent, and she wanted to sell. I advised her not to, but she sold it anyway. Within three months, the fund's price doubled. This is price fluctuation, pure and simple. A fundamentally sound investment should be held because eventually it will perform.

No investment goes up all the time. You wait because most good investments create profits for their investors eventually. Over the past 70-plus years, the stock market has risen at a double-digit average per year. That kind of long-term power you want to harness for yourself. If you hold for the long term, you don't need to be Bill Gates to make money.

A RISK-REWARD EXAMPLE

Most major issuers of debt do so in the form of bonds—corporations, states, cities, and even towns—and are rated in terms of their financial state (and therefore their ability to make good on interest and principal payments to bondholders) by several internationally reputed rating firms, most commonly, Moody's and Standard & Poor's. As an issuer's rating declines, the interest the issuer must offer to attract buyers increases. Very low or unrated bonds are "junk" bonds, which offer the highest available returns for bond buyers—and incur the most risk for buyers. They are most often issued by companies with lots of debt already, those that have fallen on hard times or just small companies whose bonds lack rating by the major rating services. Every unrated bond fits into the junk category. Companies that must cover crushing interest and principal payments on their bonds have to offer high rates of interest.

Those who buy junk bonds are less likely to get paid than investors who buy triple-A-rated bonds. Don't get me wrong. I'm not saying junk bonds are likely to default. Yet, if you bought two bonds, one junk and the other investment grade, the bond more likely to turn into a black hole is the junk, though it is probably unlikely either will default.

Investors know this, but they're willing to buy junk bonds because they demand—and get—greater rates of return and are willing to take the additional risk. Otherwise, investors would put their money into low-risk and less-enriching government bonds and be done with it. Why take a chance with a junk bond if you can get the same return with a government security? Junk bonds have at times been excellent investments, especially when the market has made them pariahs. That's when they've produced superior "devastation dividends," which I will discuss later.

Your tolerance for risk must be matched with the rewards you expect. If your financial plan requires a rate of return of 25 percent for 20 years, you better be on friendly terms with Lady Luck and expect to see her dark side once in a while. Anticipate losing money with such a plan, because to get such a high rate of return you'll have to take on a high degree of risk. If that's not acceptable, then create a plan that does not require a high rate of return and this high level of risk. A more easily attained 10 percent to 12 percent a year, for instance, allows for a financial plan carrying much less risk.

Modern Portfolio Theory

What does someone with a job on Wall Street, a loft in the trendy Soho area of Manhattan, and a portfolio of bank and brokerage firm stocks have in common with someone who owns an employment agency in Silicon Valley, has a house nearby, and invests in high-tech mutual funds?

The answer: Neither is diversified. The New Yorker's job is dependent on the financial industry, as are the values of the loft and her stock investments. The Californian lacks diversity because the employment agency is dependent on the high-tech industry, as are the values of his house and mutual funds.

There is a direct correlation between risk and diversification. Diversification accomplished through asset allocation (putting your eggs in many carefully chosen baskets), appears to offer the proverbial free lunch—high returns with lower risk. This actually happens and it's not due to alchemy. Diversification works because it helps eliminate unnecessary risk, which is any risk you can reduce without diminishing your return.

By reducing this risk, you lower your overall risk and enjoy greater rewards. Asset allocation does this by combining investments that move in different directions in similar circumstances. If interest rates go up because of inflation, bond prices fall. The losses on the bonds are made up with gains elsewhere, such as in real estate, which increases when inflation heats up.

So powerful is this theory that those who helped develop and quantify it—Harry Markowitz, William Sharpe, and Merton Miller—shared the 1990 Nobel Prize in Economics for their work in this area. The theory is often called the *Modern Portfolio Theory* because it focuses on how to allocate assets to maximize the return for a given risk level.

In the realm of investing, we face three choices:

1. Which individual investments to buy.

2. When to buy and sell—this is timing.

3. The overall mix of investments, namely, diversification or asset allocation.

If asked to rank these three in order of importance—which will have the greatest effect on how well our investments do—most people will usually say individual investments are most important. They would probably pick as the second most important, when to buy and sell (the famous "buy low, sell high" axiom). I'm sure the overall mix would come last.

The Really Stupid: Not having diversification come first.

Lower risk, better returns—that's what diversification promises. And the research proves it works. Asset allocation is the primary determinant of how well your investments will do, with market timing and security selection both playing a minor role.

Diversification is more difficult to accomplish than it appears. Financial planners like myself work hard fine tuning the portfolios we put together for our clients. This is where financial planners earn their compensation. This is how good financial planners are often able to have their clients' returns consistently outperform the overall market.

HOW MY CLIENTS' PORTFOLIOS PERFORM

Let me give you an idea of what I do for my clients. Your financial planner may do something similar, though I've spent many years studying how various investments perform in given types of markets and now use that knowledge to mix-and-match investments so a client's portfolio can reach the client's goals, with a minimum of risk.

One commonly used measure of risk for a portfolio is standard deviation. This is a common statistical concept taught to just about everyone who has ever studied statistics. I don't need to get technical here, but put simply, approximately 68 percent of a sample will be within one standard deviation of the mean. For the S&P 500, the standard deviation is about 15. The average annual return of the market is 10.3 percent. This means that 68 percent (or roughly two-thirds) of the time, you can expect the S&P mean (average) to move between 25.3 percentage points (10.3 + 15) and –4.7 (10.3 – 15). This movement is the risk you incur by investing in the stock market, as measured by the S&P 500. Risk is just another way of looking at volatility: the more volatility, the more risk, with the reverse holding true.

As an example, my clients who want a fairly low-risk portfolio, one that should produce an 8 percent to 10 percent annual return over the long term, have a standard deviation of about 5, which is one-third of the market's 15 (again, as measured by the S&P 500). Modern Portfolio Theory tells us we should be generating an annual return in the 8-to-10-percent range.

If you want a greater return, you must accept greater risk, as I discussed above, recognizing that I've been able to generate solid returns with considerably less market risk than the market overall. I'm able to get a 10 percent to 12 percent return with a standard deviation of 7 to 10, or about one-half to two-thirds of the standard deviation of the market's risk. With my most aggressive portfolios, which have an expected rate of return of 14 percent, the standard deviation is about equal to the market.

Here are benchmarks for the long-term average rate of return:

Medium-low-risk portfolio: should earn about
10 percent a year

Medium-risk portfolio: should earn about 12 percent a year (about 70 percent of my clients have this portfolio)
Aggressive portfolio: should earn about 14 percent a year

The Good: I follow my own recommendations and use the medium-risk portfolio for the vast majority of my investment assets. I believe if an investment isn't good enough for me, it isn't good enough for my clients.

The Really Stupid: Worrying about market timing and individual stocks.

Two things you should note here: 1. I'm able to generate quite solid returns with considerably less risk than the market overall. 2. The more returns you want, the greater the risk you will have to assume. Your financial planner should be able to produce risk/return scenarios fairly comparable to what I've outlined here or find yourself a new planner.

VARIOUS RISKS

Though such strategies as diversification help you avoid risk in investing, you still need to understand the various kinds of risks and how each affects your financial well being. Here are the more important kinds of risks.

Liquidity Risk
Liquidity is the ease with which an investment or financial instrument can be turned into cash. A checking account is more

liquid than a car, which is more liquid than a house, which is more liquid than a major office building. The more illiquid the investment, the harder it is to turn into cash.

A house is a classic example. Due to the difficulty of finding buyers and the trouble buyers have getting mortgages; rarely can you quickly turn a house into cash. It usually takes at least a couple of months and often much longer. That's a lack of liquidity. How much money you get for the house is also a factor, and that relates to marketability.

Illiquid investments aren't necessarily poor investments. In fact, there's evidence that investors pay a price for liquidity. After all, it's valuable, so there's no reason to think the desirability of having ready access to cash comes free.

Buying liquid investments may mean you're paying for something (liquidity) and not using it, so be sure you need it before paying for it. Even stocks can be fairly illiquid when they lack buyers. This is particularly true with smaller, obscure stocks on the over-the-counter market. Even on the New York Stock Exchange (NYSE), some stocks are more liquid than others. There are about 2,800 companies on the NYSE, many of which you've never heard of and which don't attract much trading. With such stocks, it can be difficult to get a buyer, and if you do, the price might be low because of the lack of buyers.

One academic study calculated that between 1961 and 1980 the least-liquid stocks on the NYSE averaged an 8.5 percent a year higher return than the most liquid stocks. An extension of the study for the 1980–1985 period found the least-liquid stocks outperformed the most-liquid by almost 6 percentage points a year. Those willing to buy and hold the least-liquid stocks came out significantly ahead in the long term.

What to do about liquidity risk: Use the buy-and-hold strategy; that is, plan for the long term. It minimizes liquidity risk.

Examples of illiquid investments or those it is difficult to get your money out of:

- Real estate.
- Thinly traded stocks.
- Art and collectibles.
- Precious metals.

Examples of highly liquid/easy-to-sell investments:

- Stocks of major corporations.
- Money-market mutual funds.
- Savings and checking accounts.
- All Treasuries.

Interest Rate Risk

Interest rates change, sometimes daily. The prices of bonds, mortgages, and other financial products rise and fall directly in response to interest rate changes and thus expose the investor to interest rate risk.

Investing in an asset subject to interest rate risk is a little like committing to a family picnic in uncertain weather. You can check the weather report and get a forecast for the day of your outdoor extravaganza. Likewise, you can read about the Federal Reserve and talk to pundits about what interest rates will do. But once the commitment is made—going to the park and setting up the picnic table or buying a bond—events are out of your control. You have to sit back and hang on for the ride. All you can do is hope it doesn't rain on your head or pocketbook. If it does, getting out at a good price won't be easy.

What to do about interest-rate risk: Hold the asset for the long term.

Inflation Risk

"The dollar just doesn't buy what it used to," people say. They're right, and we can blame inflation. As prices rise, each dollar buys less. Inflation risk is so important that it is a major part of our Bulletproofing protection.

What to do about inflation risk: Bulletproof.

Financial Risk

The risk that debt won't be repaid by the issuer is the financial risk that companies can and do veer suddenly toward default (just like individuals). The credit ratings of Moody's and Standard & Poor's place a lot of emphasis on this risk.

What to do about financial risk: Invest in mutual funds and variable annuities whose diversity significantly reduces this risk.

Reinvestment Risk

You're 45 years old and buy a 20-year bond that pays 10 percent. You dream about what you'll do with that steady income "guaranteed" until you retire. Think again. Many bonds have "call" features, which means the issuing company can call (redeem) the bond any time during the call period. This usually starts two years or later from the date of issue and continues until the date of maturity. Of course, the company recalls (repays) your principal plus accumulated interest. When CDs mature, the problem is similar.

An investment you must liquidate, leaving you with the need to find a new place to park your money, places you at reinvestment risk: the risk that you can't get the same return you were getting with comparable risk.

What to do about reinvestment risk: Invest in bonds that lack call features and invest in stocks.

The Really Stupid: One of the things I don't like about many bonds with call features is that they give you, the investor, a situation where heads you lose, tails you lose and if the coin lands on its edge, you break even. Here's what I mean: If interest rates go up, the value of your bonds go down—you lose. If interest rates go down, the value of your bonds go up and the issuer pays off your bonds and resells new bonds at a lower rate—again, you lose. If interest rates stay the same all the time, that's like the coin landing on its edge—you get what you expected to get.

Company-Specific Risk

The market can gyrate, interest rates can bounce off the walls, inflation can simmer or go ballistic, all of which affect the price of a stock. However, the company behind the stock counts, too. If it's a star performer, the stock usually responds. If the company stumbles, well, boulders have fallen off cliffs slower than some stocks have dropped on bad news. Call this company-specific risk. It's the risk directly attached to the performance of the individual company you invest in.

What to do about company-specific risk: Invest in mutual funds or variable annuities so you have a diversified portfolio of stocks.

Leverage Risk

Borrowing money to pay for an investment is *leveraging*. The more you borrow, the greater your leverage risk. Buying on margin, you can borrow up to 50 percent of the cost of a stock. Usually 80 or 90 percent of a real estate property's value can be borrowed, whereas commodities may require as little as 3 to 5 percent of the value to be paid with cash. Leveraged stocks are often less risky than highly leveraged real estate, which is less risky than very highly leveraged commodities. With commodities, you can quite easily lose more than you invested, which is why they are the riskiest of investments.

What to do about leverage risk: Match your risk level to your leverage. Don't borrow to pay for your investments if you're a low-risk taker. Borrow a lot if you share the same feelings about risk that rock climbers, Formula 1 racers, and skydivers do. Simply limit your borrowing to amounts you are comfortable with and can pay off from other sources if your investments don't work out.

Catastrophic Risk

Catastrophic risk is a label I coined for the risk that you'll lose everything. This was the risk that prompted me to create the Bulletproofing strategy.

Everyone is subject to potential catastrophic risk. Another 9/11-type terrorist attack, for instance, could devastate stocks, especially if it's a nuclear event. A depression, which would virtually wipe out most investors' portfolios, is to my mind a catastrophic event.

Though less likely to happen than other risks, its importance lies in its consequences. You may lose money if you invest in an illiquid asset, live through moderate inflation or buy the wrong type of interest-paying instrument. But, you also can lose *everything* in an economic catastrophe.

What to do about catastrophic risk: Bulletproof. Period.

Market Risk

Many a money manager and stock market observer has read Charles Mackay's 1841 classic treatise, *Extraordinary Popular Delusions and the Madness of Crowds.* Why? Because it discusses mass psychology and mass psychology moves markets.

Market risk is also called systematic risk. It's part of price movements that come from the whole market, the psychology underlying the entire market. If the market thinks we're heading out of a recession, stocks will go up, including stocks of companies not doing particularly well. A slide into a recession causes the market to tumble, including the stocks of very sound companies. This is market risk. The rest of the price movement relates to risks associated with the specific asset, called specific, nonsystematic or diversifiable risk.

How influential is market risk? Very, particularly when you diversify your portfolio, as I suggest. Use Bulletproofing to limit risk and get the best possible returns. Then, you can eliminate specific company risk by investing in many different companies. One study says that an investment portfolio of 30 or more common stocks eliminates so much specific risk (that is the risk associated with the specific company you're investing in), that 85 to 95 percent of all the risk left in the portfolio is market risk.

The Really Stupid: If you put all your money into one market or market segment, the risk is huge. By diversifying between markets, you can control up to 95 percent of the risk we face.

What to do about market risk: Use the asset allocation model we've discussed and hold for the long term.

The Good: Taking Reasonable Risks.

All these risks are important in a couple of ways. They highlight subtle risks we often overlook. They stimulate thinking about how you personally relate to risk.

Most of us are bigger risk takers at 17 than at 47 or 77. The younger we are, the less we know and the more time we have to make up for our mistakes. It's too bad because this results in very few of us starting to save at an early age.

Some time ago the *Federal Reserve Bulletin* reported that 43 percent of all American families took no financial risks. Of the nation's wealthiest families, though, the Fed found only 5 percent took no financial risks. These wealthy people know something important: It's almost impossible to build a sizable net worth without taking reasonable chances.

It's nice to talk about taking risk, but the energy is wasted unless you can handle taking the risk represented by your investment. *Take the level of risk you can live with so you don't panic and sell before you should.* As with goals, there is no right or wrong amount of risk for everyone. What's right is what you can and want to live with.

Being conservative can also prove quite risky. Conservative investors think securities such as Treasuries are safe havens. In a very real sense, they're not. Figures compiled by Ibbotson Associates, Chicago, as reported in *USA Today* (March 11, 2005), reveal that between 1926 and 2004, T bills returned 3.7 percent a year while large company stocks returned 10.4 percent. The problem: Inflation was about 3 percent a year during this period. What was the less risky investment? Stocks. They provided a pretax total return, including reinvested dividends, of 10.4 percent, as noted for the entire period of nearly 80 years. Playing it safe with an investment such as T bills that barely keep up with inflation is playing a high-risk game. In fact, after considering inflation and taxes, "safe" investments like CDs can produce a *negative return.* The way you deal with the risk (namely, price fluctuations) of stocks is by diversifying and holding for the long term. If history is a guide, that's actually less risky than government bonds.

The reason I recommended Treasuries earlier is that they are great for Bulletproofing. It is worth taking a part of your portfolio and putting it into Treasuries because of the protection against severe recession and depression that they provide. It is not worth putting *most* of your portfolio in these bonds because they generally don't provide an adequate return.

As for CDs, I call them "certificates of depreciation" because of their low (or even negative) return when you consider both taxes and inflation.

> **The Good: Bulletproofing is the smart way to protect yourself. You can still get good returns with very modest risk. The price fluctuations in some of the portfolios that I have designed have as little as one-third the risk of the market, while getting a return about equal to the market.**

HOW MUCH RISK CAN YOU HANDLE?

Remember that by diversifying properly, you can add investments that have a higher risk, but they may decrease your risk because they will go up and down at different times than the investments that you may already have. This is why, in some cases, Modern Portfolio Theory can increase your return and decrease your risk at the same time.

It's often hard to picture how much risk we're willing to take, so I've drawn up a risk pyramid that graphically shows how much risk different investments have in relation to one another, which is shown in Figure 5. The higher the investment is on the pyramid, the more risk—and the greater potential reward. Investments on the same level have about the same degree of risk.

How to use this pyramid:

1. What types of investments appeal to you? For most people, the desirable investments will cluster in one

Figure 5: Risk Pyramid

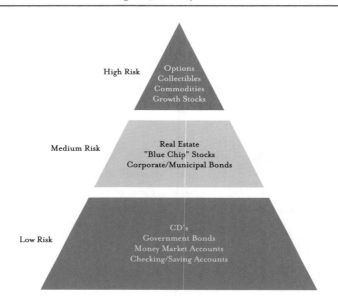

High Risk   Options
             Collectibles
             Commodities
             Growth Stocks

Medium Risk   Real Estate
              "Blue Chip" Stocks
            Corporate/Municipal Bonds

Low Risk   CD's
              Government Bonds
            Money Market Accounts
            Checking/Saving Accounts

area toward the top, middle, or bottom of the pyramid. If you like futures, speculatives and options, you like risk. Someone more attuned to collectibles, growth mutual funds, and high-grade preferred stocks is a middle-of-the road investor (most of my clients fall into this category). If you feel most comfortable with high-grade preferred stocks, money market accounts, and Treasuries, then you like little risk.

2. Structure your portfolio to match your feelings about risk. Place most of your money in the investments with the amount of risk that allows you to be comfortable.

3. This pyramid is a guideline. Just because you like no-leveraged real estate, for instance, doesn't mean

you can't take a flier with a speculative stock or limited partnership. Focus on the investments that match your needs.

RISKS ASSOCIATED WITH VARIOUS INVESTMENTS

Bonds	Interest rate risk
	Inflation risk
	Catastrophic risk
	    Inflation: Price of bonds will
	        plummet
	    Depression: Bonds won't be repaid

Certificates of Deposit	Reinvestment risk Inflation risk Catastrophic risk with inflation
Money Market Fund	Reinvestment risk Inflation risk Catastrophic risk with inflation
Treasuries	Reinvestment risk Interest rate risk Inflation risk Catastrophic risk with inflation

Stocks	Market risk
	Company-specific risk
	Liquidity risk, especially for thinly traded
	  stocks
	Catastrophic risk with depression/severe
	  recession and inflation

Real Estate	Liquidity risk Market risk Catastrophic risk with depression/severe recession
Commodities	Leverage risk Market risk Catastrophic risk with depression/severe recession
Collectibles	Liquidity risk Market risk Catastrophic risk with depression/severe recession
Precious metals	Liquidity risk Market risk Catastrophic risk with depression/severe recession

If you have any questions or require any clarification, please feel free to contact me at 800-422-9997.

MUTUAL FUNDS

THE SMART WAY TO INVEST

If you want good, long-term performance . . .

If you want to know what mutual funds are . . .

If you want to know which mutual funds are smart . . .

If you want to know the disadvantages of mutual funds . . .

You need to read this chapter.

Some time ago, I had a prospective client who got into the market at the right time but, even so, did not make money. Jonathan, who was working through a broker, came into my office very angry. He had invested in individual stocks and stock mutual funds (which are pooled funds that invest in stocks and are managed by professionals) at a time when the stock market was about to take off. Jonathan, in other words, had timed his entry into the world of investing nearly perfectly. He got in, and in a big way, just as the market was beginning a historic boom.

Good for him, you're probably thinking, but I bet you're wondering why he was angry. He had good reason to be angry because he did not make any money during the five years prior to our meeting. I don't mean that he did well but others did a lot better. I don't mean his investments just didn't keep up with the rapid rise in the market. I mean *he didn't make a cent* during five years of a bull market. He literally broke even at a time when the market more than doubled.

Even though he had the foresight to be in the market during one of the greatest bull markets in history, he lost out for two reasons: 1) He invested in poorly performing stocks and mutual funds, and 2) he made frequent trades rather than using a buy-and-hold strategy. The typical churn and burn of the big brokerage firms, i.e. buy what's hot and you are almost guaranteed to lose money. You then move to the next thing that is hot and get killed again. Just one of these mistakes can wipe out a person's profits; together they are sure to be deadly. Jonathan's investments were dead in the water.

The Bad: He lacked a game plan.

The Really Stupid: He relied on a stockbroker's recommendations. The most expensive thing in the world is bad advice and he had plenty of that.

His plan should have been to use a long-term buy-and-hold strategy. Instead, he acted more like a speculator. As for his stockbroker, he put Jonathan into stocks and funds sponsored by the broker's own firm and encouraged Jonathan to trade liberally, generating, of course, commissions for the broker.

Most major brokerage and major financial planning firms sponsor mutual funds. The problem arises because these firms sometimes have paid their brokers larger commissions to sell investors their in-house funds rather than those sponsored by other companies, or penalize them if they sell another firm's funds. In fact, in the past some firms required their brokers to push the in-house products. It's no surprise, then, that brokers push their own firm's products first. Sadly for the investor, funds sponsored by major brokerage firms are typically poor investments. Weak performers, these funds always enrich their sponsors and salespeople, but far less frequently outperform the market.

The Really Stupid: Investing in a brokerage firm's own funds.

Jonathan's situation was made worse by an especially greedy broker. Not only couldn't he pick a decent stock or fund, but he had Jonathan do a great deal of trading, generating commissions with every buy and sell order while taking away Jonathan's profits.

Within weeks of our meeting, I had Jonathan into solid consistent funds. His portfolio increased in value more than 30 percent in the following 18 months. Had he stayed with his broker, I'm sure he would have been lucky to break even during that time.

Over many years I have developed a highly effective approach to picking mutual funds and highly effective investment strategies for using them. I've simplified it here so you can use it with ease and complete confidence. By the time you finish this chapter, you'll know how to invest in mutual funds.

A CHANGE IN STRATEGY

When I wrote my book *Bulletproof Your Financial Future* in the early 1990s, I had an approach to investing I recommended to all my clients. My approach used three types of investment accounts and I prioritized them based on a tax point of view:

1. Tax deductible, tax deferred accounts, such as a 401(k) plans, pension plans, 403(b)s, SEP/IRAs and IRAs.

2. Tax-deferred accounts, such as annuities and non-deductible IRAs.

3. Taxable accounts, such as individual, joint and trust accounts.

Note: Numbers 2 and 3 might be reversed, depending on a person's situation.

Tax-deductible, tax-deferred investments were the most desirable, followed by tax-deferred, with taxable accounts as the least desirable. Times change, tax laws change, and my advice has changed. The first type of investment account I now recommend is identical to what I've always recommended, namely tax-deductible, tax-deferred accounts.

The Good: Whenever you can use the power of tax-deductible, tax-deferred investments, do so.

My Number One law of taxes: Delay. Delay. Delay. Postpone. Postpone. Postpone. Put it off. Put it off. Put it off. To win the tax game, you die before you pay the taxes. And if you're really, really good, you don't even pay them when you die. This is my goal for myself and all my clients.

What has changed is the second type. What I used to say was Number 2—tax-deferred accounts—is now down to Number 3. Your second type of account should be a taxable account.

No, I don't now think that giving money to Uncle Sam is a good idea. As much as I love our country, I don't love it enough to give it any more money than I have to. What have changed are the tax laws, and as these have changed, so has my recommended strategy. The current rate (as I am writing this book) on long-term capital gains is a low 15 percent (of course, this could change at any time). That has made taxable accounts more desirable than tax-deferred ones for most people in moderate- to high-tax brackets. You can minimize your tax burden even more by choosing mutual funds with low turnover rates. Tax-deferred accounts have negatives, such as when you take money out of them, the money is taxed as ordinary income at a fairly high rate. This is why I now favor taxable investment accounts over tax-deferred accounts. This change in strategy, of course, results in changes in where you place your money.

The Good: I recommend mutual funds instead of annuities if it is a taxable account only. If it is an IRA account, we may use annuities for a client's guarantees. I occasionally use annuities for taxable accounts if their tax rate is very close to the ordinary income tax rate. (See the annuity chapter.)

To help deal with the tax implications of annuities, I now generally recommend holding them inside an IRA. For most of my clients in moderate- to high-tax brackets, mutual funds are now the investment-vehicle-of-choice for non-IRA account assets.

Let me talk about the basics of mutual funds first, before I discuss their benefits. Realize that of all the investment vehicles available, mutual funds are likely to be the one you will use the most.

WHAT ARE MUTUAL FUNDS?

Mutual funds are investment vehicles made up of the stocks and/or bonds of various companies or government entities. A stock mutual fund invests solely in the stocks of corporations. Some specialize, such as in small companies, pharmaceutical companies or Japanese companies. There are also bond funds, which invest in bonds issued by corporations and government agencies. There are mutual funds that have a bit of both—stocks as well as bonds. In Appendix B, I cover the many different types of funds available.

The world of finance has created mutual fund companies. Some of the better-known companies are American Funds, Fidelity, Franklin Templeton and Vanguard. Such companies create, manage and market mutual funds to the investing public. Virtually all large brokerage firms, such as Merrill Lynch and Charles Schwab, offer their own mutual funds, as well as selling the offerings of various mutual fund companies. In addition, most large insurance companies offer their own mutual funds as well. Even the guy who used to be a grease monkey down the street is probably selling a mutual fund. You have to be really careful because there are thousands of funds available. We will discuss later how to be judicious in choosing the right one.

Some of these companies sell directly to the public, while others use financial advisors, stockbrokers and others to sell their funds. As an independent financial advisor, I can pick and choose among all of the various mutual fund companies and brokerage firms to find the best ones for my clients.

There is an alternative to the traditional, pre-packaged mutual funds offered by mutual fund companies: creating your own mutual fund. A lot of people try to create their own mutual funds because of perceived benefits. But whenever people do this, they get squashed. Studies have clearly shown that those who try to manage individual stocks are much less successful than those who pick good mutual funds.

The Bad: Buying individual stocks.

Private money managers claim to be able to create mutual funds specifically for their clients, but in reality, they usually use all the same stocks for everyone and trade a lot more often than they claim. This often happens when brokers try to create mutual funds for individuals, but lack the training to do so effectively. The basic training for a mutual fund manager is someone with the designation of certified financial analyst. I don't know of a single certified financial analyst working as a stockbroker today. In other words, stockbrokers are totally incompetent for the job and you should not be doing individual stock picking in the first place. What you should really be focused on is where 95 percent of your return comes from, and that is from which markets you choose and how much money you put in those markets. In other words, don't put all your eggs in one basket. How many baskets you need and how many eggs you need in each basket are the more important questions.

WHY MUTUAL FUNDS

"There's strength in numbers," goes the adage, and that's true with mutual funds. These ever-popular financial instruments capitalize on the idea that individual investors have a hard time beating the market by themselves because of high costs, the difficulty in investing in more than a few stocks (they lack the large amount of money needed to have substantial investments in many stocks), and bad advice. If they pool their resources, however, they can hire the best money managers in the world who know how to pick winners, thereby gaining the advantages enjoyed by the big boys.

This is a very appealing scenario. So appealing, in fact, that trillions of dollars are invested in mutual funds. There are solid reasons why mutual funds are so popular. These include:

1. Diversification: Mutual funds are an easy way to build a diversified portfolio (which makes them a valuable tool

for Bulletproofing) because they invest in dozens, even hundreds of stocks, which creates far more diversification than almost any individual investor could achieve by him or herself. As we've learned, diversification, properly done, increases returns while limiting risks.

2. Professional management: Fund managers are typically seasoned professionals. They've studied the market for years; have enjoyed success as investors; have information, personnel, and technology at their disposal to exploit the best investments and provide individual investors with access to sophisticated portfolio management only the superrich can afford on their own.

3. Access to markets: Mutual funds have access to markets not readily open to individual investors. This is particularly true of foreign markets, where it is very difficult for individuals to get accurate information and even to buy and sell stocks.

4. Fund families: Individual funds usually come bundled as one in a "family of funds" by their sponsor. Several mutual funds are offered, each with its own investment objectives and management team. The American Funds Group, for example, numbers among its funds: American Balanced Fund, American High-Income Municipal Bond Fund, EuroPacific Growth Fund, Fundamental Investors, Growth Fund of America, The New Economy Fund, SmallCap World Fund, Tax Exempt Bond Fund of America, Tax Exempt Fund of California, U.S. Government Securities Fund and Washington Mutual Investors Fund. You can switch between them at no cost. While you don't want to switch because you think one fund is likely to be hotter than another, you do at times need to move around a portion of your assets to maintain balance in your portfolio and to maintain your Bulletproof protection according to our asset allocation model.

5. Liquidity: Cashing in your shares in mutual funds is easy, so there's ready access to your money. This liquidity is a valuable benefit of mutual funds. Bookkeeping for tax purposes is simple because the fund does the work. And the fund will automatically reinvest your dividends and capital gains if you want.

6. A source of income: Funds also can be a source of income, as you can withdraw money when you wish. This will limit your profitability, of course, but a good fund will be a star performer even when factoring in regular withdrawals.

7. Buy a sector: You can buy oil, so that you have a piece of almost everyone in the oil business without buying a single oil company.

8. Some foreign stocks sell in such huge blocks, like a million dollars at a time, average investors have no chance to buy them unless they use a mutual fund that can afford to buy huge blocks.

DISADVANTAGES

While mutual funds have many advantages, they do come with some disadvantages. One is that they charge sales and management fees. We'll discuss these in a moment. Let's just say that nothing of value in life is free, so if you expect to get good investment advice and sound management from a fund for free, you are being unrealistic.

Another disadvantage is that they're usually taxable. Dividends are now taxed as capital gains rates and interest is taxed at ordinary income tax rates. Even worse, if a mutual fund sells stocks it made money on and doesn't offset these gains with the sale of stocks that had losses, you might find yourself in the unenviable situation of paying taxes even when the overall value of your mutual fund has declined. There are, of course, exceptions, such as mutual funds that are in tax-advantaged accounts, such as 401(k)s, IRAs and annuities. Another exception is funds that invest in tax-advantaged types of investments, such as municipal bonds.

Performance is another potential shortcoming. With all the money, professional management and computers at their disposal, one would think mutual funds would be stellar performers. A few are, and these I focus on in my financial planning practice. But, actually, most are not. *The Wall Street Journal* (May 3, 2004) reported: "At the start of this year [2004], the investment performance of more than 70 percent of actively managed U.S. stock funds trailed that of the Standard & Poor's 500 stock index during the past decade." Put another way, more than 70 percent of mutual funds that are actively managed (meaning they are not indexed, such as to the S&P or Dow Jones Industrials) cannot match the performance of the market overall, let alone beat it.

In theory, index funds look good. That's because most investors believe index funds will give the return earned by the indexes they follow. But they don't. Their costs preclude them from matching the performance of the index. Of course, good mutual funds, such as those offered by American Funds, consistently outperform the indexes—let alone index funds. You generally will do much better with a good, actively managed fund than any index fund. For that reason, I never have my clients invest in index funds.

The costs of running a fund dictate that a manager has to have better-than-average returns just to stay even with the market. This accounts for the popularity of index funds. These try to mirror the stocks in various indices, such as the Standard & Poor's 500. The S&P 500 tracks price movements of 500 major corporations and is used by many on Wall Street as a measurement of how the stock market is moving overall. An S&P

Index fund just puts money into those stocks that make up the index. The idea is, if you basically have the stocks that comprise an index, you'll do about as well as the index. Note: There may be some variation from the index's performance because there are costs involved with managing and marketing any fund, including index funds. Also, there may be some lag when the stocks making up an index change, which happens with some frequency, especially in a large index like the S&P 500.

It makes you wonder why you need a manager; an investment novice could manage an index fund, at least in theory. Yet, you should not invest in index funds.

The Good: Buy solid performing actively managed mutual funds. They will outperform any index fund and you will, in the long run, generally make more money.

The Bad: Index funds always under-perform the indexes they follow because of the costs of running them.

The Really Stupid: Index funds because they are even more expensive than their cheaper alternative, the exchange-traded fund.

Well-managed funds do well. The *Journal of Financial Planning* (October 2005, p. 54) said: "An analysis of investment return data from January 1975 through June 2004 shows actively managed U.S. equity funds performed better than the S&P 500 two-thirds of the time and by an average of 2 percent annually. Using both Modern Portfolio Theory and behavioral finance

measurements, the investors in actively managed funds appear
to have taken less actual risk than the index."

The reason the actively managed funds beat the indexes in
the study is because someone finally had the common sense to
weigh the funds by how much was invested in them. In the past,
a rinky-dink fund with fifty million dollars in it would be
counted as much as a fund like the Growth Fund of America,
which has around one hundred billion dollars in it. To get the
2 percent that the study talks about, you weigh investments by
where people invest their money and take that average against
the index. An average of 2 percent annually is a huge amount
over the long-term.

Another potential challenge to mutual funds is their pro-
liferation. When a fund firm is very popular, it has to open new
funds. One consequence of this is the irony that there are more
stock mutual funds than individual stocks. The more funds a
firm has, the harder its management challenges become. It is
harder to manage a dozen funds than a half dozen, and some
of the larger fund companies have dozens of funds. The Vanguard Group has about 90 funds and Fidelity Investments has
more than 150.

My favorite fund group is American Funds, which I've been
recommending on my radio program, in my writings, and to
my clients since the 1980s, which was long before most financial advisors had ever heard of this fund company. Founded in
1931, American Funds has—because of its track record rather
than its marketing (they do not advertise)—become the largest
mutual fund family in America, if you don't count money market accounts (and is ranked number 2 if you do count them).
Yet, even though it has become so large, it still has a fraction of
the funds that other large fund families have. It has 29 U.S.
funds, which is about 20 percent of the number of funds that
Fidelity has and one-third that of Vanguard. Franklin Templeton Investments, another large fund family, offers more than

200 investment products globally. They have maintained the integrity of the funds by buying companies like Templeton Funds and kept the same management teams in place. Each team still uses its own approach separately from the other teams. So this is like a group of small mutual fund companies instead of a huge one with a few good managers scattered among them. They have been very effective over the past 10 years and have ranked second only to American Funds in their performance as a fund family.

Full disclosure: John Templeton endorsed my first book and has been kind enough to be on my radio show more than anyone else. I rarely have guests on, but when I do, they are of very high caliber like Sir John. The reason he endorsed my book and has been on my radio show is because we share the same approach to the investment world, which is that we believe in buying investments that are relatively low in cost compared to other investments and holding them for the long term.

The Good: American Funds and Franklin Templeton are great mutual fund families because of their discipline developed over many years, which has become part of their corporate culture and assures consistency over the long term.

You should ask yourself: How many of these funds can be productive especially when there aren't that many proven managers available to manage them? Maybe one or two or a handful will prove to be adequate performers and if you happen to invest in these, you will come out okay. Chances are, you'll get one or more of the dogs, because most funds are relatively poor performers.

The Bad: Investing in funds from sponsoring firms that have many funds, because the numbers are working against you.

The Really Stupid: Investing in funds sponsored by large brokerage firms.

Cost is another consideration, although not as significant a concern as many investors think and the media would like you to believe. The ways mutual funds charge is almost as varied as the number of mutual funds in existence. There are, however, some basic methods by which funds charge their customers. Among them are:

No-load funds. Some funds sell direct to the public. They may do so via direct mail or through an Internet site. These funds do not carry a sales charge (or a very low one) because there are no salespeople involved in the process. Such funds are called *no-load funds.* A no-load fund is one that typically has a sales charge of 2 percent or less. Local bookstores carry books that discuss and list no-load funds. Look for websites that list no-load funds as well.

Load funds. They may charge up to the maximum sales charge allowable by the Financial Industry Regulatory Authority (FINRA), namely, 8.5 percent, though today, the maximum sales charge you are likely to see is 5.75 percent. Load funds typically are sold by financial advisors and stockbrokers. Also, the more you buy, the less the percentage load you will pay. If you are relatively affluent, you could end up paying pretty low fees, even for load funds. American Funds charges 0 percent commission even though it is a load-fund family, per se, provided you invest $1 million or more. American Funds also has no-loads available through financial advisors.

Back-end loads used to be fairly common; today, a lot less so. If you encounter a back-end load, it will probably start at 5 percent and drop 1 percent a year until it disappears altogether in five years. I think that in the future, few, maybe no, funds will have back-end loads.

Somewhat similar to the back-end charge is the redemption fee. This is paid when money is withdrawn. The difference between a back-end charge and a redemption fee is that the back-end is a sales commission paid to the person who sold you the fund. The redemption charge generally goes to the fund, and is designed to encourage investors to stay with the fund.

Adding to the confusion is the so-called 12b-1 fee. When a fund firm adopts a 12b-1 fee, it can use fund assets to pay for overhead and marketing expenses, such as advertising and sales commissions paid to brokers. This may be in addition to any commissions paid to brokers. Unlike the load charges, which are paid by the investor just once, 12b-1 charges are paid annually. The advantage of 12b-1 fees is that they motivate your broker to provide personal service and with good brokers, it really does work that way.

Front-load and back-load funds are also known as A and B shares, respectively. These are considered different classes of shares. If you purchase A shares, you pay a sales load upfront—that is, at the time you purchased the shares. Your annual expense ratio, however, would be lower than most other share classes, largely because A shares generally charge a 12b-1 fee of no more than 0.25 percent. Also, with A shares, generally the larger your purchase, the lower the percent you pay in commissions. With American Funds' Growth Fund of America, if you invest less than $25,000, you get charged 5.75 percent; if you invest more than $250,000, the commission is only 2.5 percent.

Back-loaded funds usually have the "B" share class designation. With these, you don't pay a sales load upfront when you buy, but you do when you sell, though as just noted, this fee declines over time until it disappears. With this fee model, there's generally a higher annual expense ratio than with A shares. B shares usually have very high 12b-1 fees of 1 percent, and a big portion of that 12b-1 fee goes to pay brokers' commissions.

The Really Stupid: Buying B shares. With B shares, there are no breakpoints, no volume discounts. I have never sold a B-share mutual fund. B-shares are typically sold by the big brokerage firms, which is yet another reason to avoid them.

The mutual funds that I use in my portfolios have either some or all no-load mutual funds due to the fact that they are usually the cheapest for the investor. Here is what the Securities and Exchange Commission (SEC) says on its website about no-load funds: "Some funds call themselves 'no-load.' As the name implies, this means that the fund does not charge any type of sales load . . . however, not every type of shareholder fee is a 'sales load,' and a no-load fund may charge fees that are not sales loads. For example, a no-load fund is permitted to charge purchase fees, redemption fees, exchange fees, and account fees, none of which is considered to be a 'sales load.' In addition, under FINRA rules, a fund is permitted to pay its annual operating expenses and still call itself 'no-load,' unless the combined amount of the fund's 12b-1 fees or separate shareholder service fees exceeds 0.25 percent of the fund's average annual net assets."

In May 2004, a Morningstar analyst posted a column entitled, "Don't Rule Out Load Funds." In it, she wrote: "We here at Morningstar acknowledge that there are plenty of investors who prefer the guidance and support of a broker or financial advisor. Thus, Morningstar doesn't criticize load funds simply because they charge a sales fee. While it's true that most load investors will pay more in total costs than those who invest in comparable no-load offerings, load investors are paying for the extra service and guidance, while no-load investors typically go it alone."

An article in the May 3, 2004, issue of *The Wall Street Journal,* looked at past performance and fees as ways to pick fund winners. It says: "Because a fund that keeps tight control over expenses has a built-in advantage over an identical fund with higher costs, many investors think that low-cost funds are destined to be winners more often than their more-expensive counterparts."

"The only problem: Both strategies [looking at past performance and fees] are largely bunk in many cases."

The article goes on to say: " . . . low fees were useful in picking winners in only some cases, while in others, higher fees were actually more dependable indicators of top returns down the road."

I've seen statistics that say the funds whose expenses are among the highest one-third outperform those funds whose expenses are in the lower one-third. Again, you often get what you pay for.

The Good: Look at a fund's long-term track record, not its fees. It's the track record that counts. Never forget: It's all about performance, performance and performance. It is how much you get, not how much you pay, that is important.

Below is a breakpoint schedule for A-Share mutual fund purchases:

Amount of Fund Family Purchased Per Household	Sale Charge
American Funds—Equity Funds	
Less than $25,000	5.75%
$25,000 but less than $50,000	5.00%
$50,000 but less than $100,000	4.50%
$100,000 but less than $250,000	3.50%
$250,000 but less than $500,000	2.50%
$500,000 but less than $750,000	2.00%
$750,000 but less than $1,000,000	1.50%
$1,000,000 or more	0.00%

More significant are the annual management fees or expenses all funds charge, typically about 1.5 percent for a U.S. stock fund per year. Some, though, are as low as one-half of 1 percent. My favorite mutual fund family, as I've already mentioned, is American Funds, which has very low management fees, though, of course, it charges an upfront sales commission. Yet, even with this commission, its funds are still cheaper than many no-load funds over the long term because its ongoing management fees are lower. Let's say the difference in management fees is 1 percent a year. In this case, you will make up the sales commission (2.5 percent) in two and a half years. And, since you're holding your funds for the long-term and therefore likely keeping them for more than six years, the load funds from this family of funds turns out to be cheaper than the no-load funds over the long term.

The Good: Look at performance, not fees.

The Bad: Thinking no-loads always give you better returns. Sometimes that is true; sometimes it is not true.

In addition, if you only looked at cost when choosing a mutual fund, you'd never pick a foreign stock fund because they have significantly higher costs than domestic stock funds. You would lose the increased rate of return and diversification foreign stock funds bring to your portfolio.

The bottom line: It's not what you pay in commissions and management fees that count—it's how well the fund performs.

Typically, when you read rankings of funds provided by a number of publications and websites, they discount fees and commissions from the funds' rates of return, so the returns you read about are *after* the fees. If a load fund has provided a 10 percent annual return on average for the past 10 years, and a no-load provided a 7 percent annual return on average for the past 10 years, the performance of both funds were likely calculated *after* deducting fees and commissions. In this case, why would you buy the no-load? The load outperformed the no-load, even after taking into account its higher upfront costs. This is something I've seen happen many times. It's what *The Wall Street Journal* was talking about in the article quoted above.

The Good: Recognize that sometimes you get what you pay for.

I know investment advisors who are both honest and competent who charge commissions. I also know investment advisors who are honest and competent who don't charge commissions. The key is not how someone charges, but how good they are at what they do. What do they deliver at the end of the day? What rate of return have they given you over the years? If it is great, who cares what they charge? I have had clients tell me that they don't care how much I charge as long as I keep doing what I'm doing.

> **The Good: The key is competence. Not how or even how much someone charges.**

The bottom line is, I believe the smartest way to invest is with mutual funds. The problem is that there are a lot of really bad mutual funds out there, but the good news is there are plenty of great ones as well. If you follow my approach to picking mutual funds, you should end up with good ones as well or you can call and get a free copy of my Bruce's Best Mutual Funds by calling my office at 800-422-9997.

How I Pick the Mutual Fund Winners

Finding the Best of the Best

If you want to have only the best mutual funds . . .

If you want to know how to avoid the mutual funds that are likely to fall, even if their current record is good . . .

If you want to only have the best of the best as part of your investments . . .

You need to read this chapter.

The Investment Company Institute (www.ici.org) is the national association of the investment company industry, and it publishes a great deal of data and information pertaining to mutual funds. The ICI breaks down mutual funds into four basic types:

1. Equity (also called stock) mutual funds, which invest in stocks

2. Bond mutual funds, which invest in bonds

3. Hybrid mutual funds, which invest in stocks, bonds and sometimes other securities

4. Money market funds, which invest in securities, such as bonds, that mature in about one year or less

Equity, bond and hybrid mutual funds are called long-term funds because they invest in securities that mature after more than one year or, as with stocks, do not have a maturity aspect to them.

As of the last numbers I've seen, of the total money invested in mutual funds, 42 percent was invested in equity funds, 18 percent was invested in bond funds, 5 percent in hybrid funds and 36 percent in money market funds.

You have to be very careful when investing in mutual funds, because there are so many to choose from. That's why I recommend you call me to get my Bruce's Best list of mutual funds before you buy any fund. I'd include my list in this book, but I continually update it, which means it may be out of date by the time you read this book.

MUTUAL FUND'S INVESTMENT PHILOSOPHY

Funds come in many different flavors, focusing on very different kinds of investments, and that's why they fit in everyone's portfolio. Use them to tailor your investments to match your needs. For example, if you need inflation protection, you might buy a gold or real estate fund. Need to diversify outside the country? Try a foreign stock fund. Also, mutual funds are perfect vehicles for dollar-cost averaging because fund sponsors allow shareholders to invest as little as $25 at a time.

You make money in stocks in two ways: dividends (typically cash paid to shareholders that comes from a company's profits) and capital appreciation (when the stock price increases). The two general categories of stock mutual funds—growth and income—mirror this in their payoffs. A growth fund's investment strategy is to buy the stocks of companies likely to grow and, hopefully, see their stock price grow with them. Stocks in growth-stock mutual funds usually pay small or no dividends. Income funds, on the other hand, seek to provide their shareholders with income now.

They like companies that pay sizable dividends, such as utilities and companies in mature, low-growth industries.

There are variations within these categories. Growth funds might invest in established high-tech firms, like Microsoft and Oracle. These companies may pay small dividends, but plow much of their earnings back into research and development rather than paying out much of their earnings to shareholders. Other funds are more speculative. Some, for instance, invest in small-company stocks of young and unproven firms. The fund's prospectus, as well as write-ups by Morningstar, Williamson and various business periodicals, will tell you what a fund's objectives are.

In addition to stock funds, there are also money market funds, which invest in short-term investments, pay low rates of return, and are very safe in maintaining the value of your principal; bond funds, which invest in government bonds and/or the bonds of major corporations; tax-exempt bond funds, which put their money into municipal and other vehicles that are exempt from federal (and sometimes state and local) income taxes; and balanced funds, which include stocks and bonds in their portfolios.

Bonds and Bond Funds

We buy long-term treasuries for protection and they never leave the portfolio, unless there is a terrible crisis and they skyrocket in value, then we would sell them down to their recommended level. Whereas with bond funds, the manager decides the maturity of the bonds and the mix of the bonds and sometimes you just let them run it when interest rates are going up or down. When interest rates are going down, they tend to shorten up so that they don't have losses and when the interest rates get to a nice high level, they lock in long-term bonds and give us a good rate of return over the long term.

You can invest in bonds by buying them outright or buying shares of a mutual fund, which, in turn, buys and holds the bonds themselves. Note: We don't use Treasury bond funds. We use individual Treasury bonds because we don't want the bond fund manager deciding what term Treasury bond we have.

For information on how bonds fluctuate, please refer to the Depression chapter.

The Really Stupid: Municipal bonds with call features.

Many bonds, especially municipal bonds, have call features, which allow the company or agency that issued the bond to call, redeem, or cash in the bond at a certain date before its maturity for a certain price. If a bond pays 8 percent and the current market rate is 4 percent—and the bond is callable—the issuer will, whenever possible, call the bond and immediately turn around and sell new bonds at the lower (4 percent) rate. This is analogous to a homeowner refinancing his mortgage when interest rates drop significantly, only in this case the issuer is the one who benefits. You cannot win on municipal bonds if they have a call feature. Do not buy municipal bonds with call features.

The reason there are rating services for bonds but not stocks is because the ratings services study the issuing companies or agencies to determine the likelihood that the interest will be paid on a timely basis over the life of the bond and the principal returned at maturity. There's nothing like this to study with stocks, because stocks don't promise interest or the return of principal. For bonds, the lower the rating, the greater the chance the bond will default on its interest payments and principal.

CLOSED- VERSUS OPEN-END FUNDS

Closed- and open-end mutual funds are two types of mutual funds worth mentioning. Closed-end funds sell a set number of shares at an initial public offering and then the shares trade like common stock, moving up and down in value with changes in the value of the fund's investments (what they buy with all the money from selling the shares).

The Bad: Closed-end funds that are selling at a premium.

Frequently, closed-end funds sell at less than their true value, or net asset value, especially immediately after they are sold to the public. If a fund has assets worth $10 million and has 1 million shares outstanding, each share has a net asset value of $10. It's not uncommon for such shares to sell at less than $10. Never buy closed-end funds at their initial offering because the chances are excellent they'll soon go down in price.

The more common open-end funds lack a finite number of shares. They issue shares when investors buy and redeem shares (buy them back) when investors sell. What investors pay and receive depends on the net asset value of the shares that day. In this case, the price is always identical to the net asset value at the time of the trade. I recommend this type of fund.

When to Use Mutual Funds

Mutual funds are useful in almost all financial situations—for retirement, estate planning, and if you need money for ongoing expenses. They are useful if you are a high-, medium- or low-risk investor. And they are of value no matter your age. Let me put it this way: Mutual funds are the most versatile investment vehicle available. That's because they are economical (their costs to the investor are modest), often effective (they are professionally managed) and varied (there are thousands), meaning you have enough choices to be able to choose the funds that really meet your needs and desires.

HOW I SELECT MUTUAL FUNDS

While I obviously like mutual funds, I've also been quite clear that you have to watch what you buy because there are many mutual funds that do not perform well—and probably never will. I've whittled down the selection process to two primary factors.

Long-Term Track Record—What's Hot Is What's Not

First, look at the fund's long-term track record. Over and over I've emphasized the importance of the buy-and-hold strategy in this book. Nowhere is this truer than with mutual funds.

The Good: Pay attention to a fund's track record.

The Really Stupid: Only pay attention to fees, while ignoring the fund's overall performance.

People think I'm crazy when I say they should have investment horizons of 10 or 20 or 30 years, or more. If they're in their 50s or 60s or 70s, such long time horizons do not seem to make sense to them this late in life.

Think again. Today, if you are a woman who is 65 years old, you can expect to live another 20 or so years, while a 65-year-old man can expect to live about 17 more years. These figures, which come from the National Center for Health Statistics are, of course, averages. If your investment horizon is a year or two or even five, what happens when the year or two is over? Or five years is over? You are back to square one. If you are in your 60s, you'll again need places to put your money given present life expectancies. If you do that, you'll have to spend all your spare time looking for investments. I find it far more productive—and profitable—to say, "I'm probably going to be around for "X" number of years, so I need investments that will take care of me that long."

I emphasize the importance of a long-term investment horizon because it directly affects how I analyze mutual funds and how I think you should.

> **The Good: Realize that you are likely to invest for the long-term, even if you think that you may not.**

Look at a fund's track record over at least 10 and preferably 15 years. I didn't just pick these numbers because I do well with them in Las Vegas. You need to look at performance over a sufficient period to see how a fund will do over good times and bad. A good 15-year track record limits your risk exposure. You might hold a fund for 20 or 30 years and want to use that as a yardstick, but not many funds have track records that long. Many have 10-year track records and these numbers are generally readily available. To get numbers for 15 years is more work. Funds usually publish figures for 1, 3, 5 and 10 years, but not 15. Getting a fund's 15-year record will usually mean calling the fund and asking for it.

The Really Stupid: Using the ratings published by the popular press.

Ratings of mutual funds, widely published in the popular press, are useless. They usually focus on the past five years or worse, the past quarter, which is not only ridiculous, but dangerous. Such ratings imply the top fund for the past quarter or past year will be at the top in the future. That's garbage. Market conditions usually cause a particular fund to be the year's stellar performer. Because these conditions constantly change, there's about as much chance of this year's number 1 fund repeating this feat year after year as there is that the federal government will never again run a deficit.

According to a study by Franklin Templeton, if you invest this year in what was last year's best market segment, not only will you not do as well as those who happened to invest in this segment last year, but you'll do worse than most investors: investing in last year's winners typically results in a return 7 percent *below the market* the following year. Let me say that again: If you invest this year in what was hot last year, you will likely do worse than the market this year—by 7 percent.

Avoid anything that's scalding at the moment. Keep in mind a favorite homily: What's hot is what's not. When something's hot, the moment to buy at the good price has already passed.

There are a few good sources for information about mutual fund performances:

1. From the funds themselves. You'd have to contact many funds to learn about their performance, but you can get long-term track record information from the funds.

2. A good book is *The 100 Best Mutual Funds You Can Buy,* by Gordon K. Williamson, published by Adams Media Corpo-

ration, with a list price of $14.95. The book can be bought at your local bookstore or online, and is updated periodically.

> **The Good: And—let's not be modest—there's Bruce's Best Mutual Funds. Give me a call. The list is free. And it is constantly updated.**

Watch Out for Rating Agencies

Morningstar and the other mutual fund rating services may give a fund its highest rating even if the manager, who was the one who made it successful, left yesterday. That's no way to choose a fund. Morningstar is fine for basic information about mutual funds, but don't pay attention to its ratings.

Motley Fool: They are truly fools. For example, they were recommending high-tech stocks at the top of the high-tech bubble. I rarely listen to them, but many of my clients have complained to me about them and how they tend to go for the latest-and-greatest trend. To my mind, that's no way to pick investments.

Management

Mutual funds, more than any other institution in the financial world, are the creation of a personality, the manager who gives the fund its character. There is in fact a "star" system, where every fund seeks to create (or steal) a star manager in the hope that he or she will produce a great track record and attract investors. Funds even lure managers from competitors with seven-figure annual incomes. If the manager likes the idea of holding cash when things in the market are murky, the fund often will be heavy with CDs and short-term bonds. In the same situation, another manager might go for blue chip stocks. It's a matter of personality.

The role of the manager was never more clearly seen than when the redoubtable Peter Lynch announced his retirement from Fidelity Investments' Magellan Fund, the largest mutual fund of its time. The announcement, made on March 28, 1990, that he would retire two months later made the front pages nationally. It was *The Wall Street Journal's* lead story, which began with the question: "How do you replace a legend?"

This is Wall Street's equivalent of Hollywood. The movie industry pays Brad Pitt and Nicole Kidman big bucks on the assumption they'll bring in millions just on their name appeal. It's the same with music, sports and publishing. Put Stephen King's name on a book, and it will sell. Have Shaquille O'Neal play on a basketball court, and people will pay to see him.

The problem is that if you invest in a fund with a star at its helm and the star then goes off to greener pastures, what do you do? I agree with an analyst quoted in *The Wall Street Journal* who said, "If the star leaves, the whole track record becomes invalid." When the star leaves, so should you.

> **The Good: If a fund relies on one manager, recognize that the fund's record is valid as a measure of its quality only as long as that manager is at its helm.**

Keep in mind: the industry average for a fund manager to be in place is 2.5 years, which is not long enough to even measure their performance and we would not use a mutual fund with management with a track record that short. The average length that managers have been at the helm of Fidelity funds is 1.5 years and at American Funds, 23 years. Guess where I prefer to invest?

We used the First Eagle Sogen Funds when one manager was there. He was replaced by someone who started doing a lot of options that were not done previously, which is completely against my philosophy as the correct way to buy a hedge investment, so we quit using it.

In fact, you're better off not putting yourself in this position in the first place. Not all funds rely principally on one person. My favorite fund families, American Funds and Franklin Templeton, do not. Fund families like these have a committee or modified committee structure. American Funds uses multiple managers for their management structure. Each fund is divided into segments, which have individual managers. Depending on the size and scope of the fund, there can be eight to 15 managers at each fund. This means that if a manager leaves, the management of the whole fund doesn't change. Some fund families like Franklin Templeton use a committee. Every fund manager, assistant manager and analyst is on the investment committee and any stock used by anyone on the investment committee must be approved by the entire investment committee. This way, the discipline stays in place. This is the key with both American Funds' and Franklin Templeton's tremendous success.

I said there were two important factors to consider when analyzing funds. That's true, but I also consider several more factors when looking at funds, and you might want to use them if you decide to do your own analysis.

INTEGRITY

I consider integrity in examining any of the mutual funds that I propose to use. I generally find when an organization is

highly disciplined, as American Funds and the Templeton portion of Franklin Templeton, that integrity is not an issue. In
fact, during the mutual fund scandal, American Funds was held
up as the example of how mutual funds families should be run.
Again, look for discipline in the investment approach such as
the multiple manager approach American Funds and Templeton use and you will usually find integrity as well.

THOSE WHO AVOID THE DOGS

I avoid funds that had sizable positions in some of the no-
table dogs of recent years. You know the dogs I'm referring
to—Enron, K-mart, Adelphia, Worldcom. If a fund manager
doesn't know a company is cooking its books, if a fund manager
can't tell when corporate management is lying to the public—
then you don't want that fund manager picking stocks for you.
Funds that lose considerable money on any major company that
goes into bankruptcy are funds to avoid.

TURNOVER RATES

Turnover rates may seem to relate to a fast food restaurant
and its revolving door of employees, here today and gone tomorrow. But with mutual funds, turnover is a little understood
but important indicator of a fund manager's philosophy.

A fund's turnover rate refers to the number of times the investment portfolio is bought and sold annually. If a fund holds
150 stocks and at any time during the previous year bought
and sold 90 stocks, its turnover rate is 60 percent (90/150).
On average, this fund trades 60 percent of its stocks a year.

Note that many of the published rankings do not include
trading expenses when they rank funds. The full costs of high
turnover rates therefore can be obscured.

A turnover rate of 200 percent in a stock fund is way too high. The more a stock fund trades, the more it resembles a speculator rather than an investor.

> **The Bad: Recognize that though you may hold a fund's stock for years, if that fund is a speculator, so are you.**

I keep emphasizing the benefits of the buy-and-hold strategy, and this principle applies to mutual fund management as well as individual investors. Some funds, if their investment philosophy is aggressive (and you know this from reading the prospectus), can have a turnover of as much as 150 percent, and that might be okay. Generally, don't go with a fund whose turnover rate is more than 150 percent. For most funds, though, the turnover rate you should prefer is 30 percent or less.

You may think that because the fund's manager is a "professional," it's okay if he or she trades a lot, they must know what they're doing. Take that with a grain of salt. There are statistics on how much funds tend to turn over their portfolios and here are some comments from those who have carefully watched this phenomenon in mutual funds.

An excerpt of John C. Bogle's book, *Common Sense on Mutual Funds,* which appeared on Yahoo's website, says: "Twenty-five years ago, fund portfolio turnover averaged 30 percent; today, it averages nearly 90 percent. Individual investors may hold stocks for decades, and families may hold them for generations, but mutual funds are rushing to buy and sell their stocks with seemingly carefree abandon based on transitory changes in prices and without concern for tax consequences. This behavior sharply reduces the returns generated for their taxable owners."

Consumer Reports in May 2004 said the turnover rate for the average stock fund was 126 percent.

Morningstar in 2003 said the average turnover rate of bond funds was 159 percent (meaning that the funds' portfolio turned over more than one-and-a-half times every year).

In 1999, Morningstar reported the following statistics:

- Five-year return for U.S. stock funds with turnovers above 174 percent: a 17.14 percent a year compounded rate of return.

- Five-year return for U.S. stock funds with turnovers less than 44 percent: an 18.75 percent a year compounded rate of return.

- Five-year return for U.S. stock funds with turnovers less than 22 percent: a 19.68 percent a year compounded rate of return.

What these numbers reveal is: The lower the turnover, the better the returns.

Besides what the turnover rate reveals about the fund manager's investment strategy, there is another reason to pay close attention to this number: It can cost you a lot of money. When you read about a fund's expenses, such as its expense ratio, the numbers don't include trading costs. These costs include such things as brokers' commissions, for buying and selling stocks and bonds, as well as other charges.

Consumer Reports, in May 2004, quoted a Morningstar executive as saying: "You never have to write a check for trading costs, but the money is seamlessly removed from your total rate of return." One study found that 100 out of 3,753 funds studied rang up higher charges for buying and selling securities than for the fund's expenses.

Consumer Reports says a study of the cost of owning the 30 most widely held domestic equity funds found, "As much as 43 percent of a mutual fund's expenses are not included in expense ratios." It cited one fund managed by one of the largest fund companies as having a listed expense ratio of 0.84 percent, but when trading costs and brokerage commissions were added, the total came to 1.64 percent.

Not only do turnover rates potentially affect costs, they may affect performance. "Excessive trading affects returns as well as cost," notes *Consumer Reports*.

With all these caveats, you can now understand why I always look at turnover rates.

LIQUIDATION RATE

I also always look at a fund's liquidation rate. This is the statistic that tells you the rate at which people leave a given mutual fund. This becomes particularly important in a down market, because that's when investors are most likely to leave a mutual fund. When people start bailing out of a fund, the manager has to sell stocks to raise the money to cash-out those leaving. This typically happens when stocks are low. This behavior on the part of fund owners forces managers to sell when stocks are low (with the reverse also being true, namely that managers have to buy when stocks are high if the fund attracts a lot of investors).

I always look for funds with low liquidation rates because its investors believe in the fund's management and don't panic when the market tanks. You want steady investors in a fund so the manager is not forced to sell when the market is down and buy when it is up.

THE BETA

The beta is a statistical technique used to measure a stock or fund's volatility compared with the market as a whole. If the fund has a beta of 1.0, then its price moves in tandem with the

market. A 10 percent increase or decrease in the market will result in a 10 percent increase or decrease in the fund's value. A
beta of 0.8 says a 10 percent change in the market results in an
8 percent (8 percent is 0.8 of 10 percent) change in the fund.
A beta of 1.2 results in a 12 percent change in the fund if the
market changes 10 percent. Obviously the higher the beta the
more volatile and risky the investment is.

For mutual funds, this is how I rank betas:

0.7 or less	Low risk
0.8–1.1	Medium risk
1.2 and up	High risk

Morningstar reports betas. Your library, financial planner,
or stockbroker should have Morningstar's reports. Or, you can
purchase information from Morningstar directly.

I discussed earlier how to assess your affinity toward risk. If
you are a low-, medium-, or high-risk investor, then orient
your mutual fund investing to funds with comparable betas.
You don't have to follow the betas religiously, however. If
you're a low-risk investor, putting some money into higher-
risk investments is okay as long as you don't bail out when the
market turns against you (as it inevitably will). Just use the
betas as a guideline.

If you are retired, having a small price fluctuation in your
total portfolio is very important because if the investments go
way down you are going to be eating the seed corn and may not
recover. You generally want investments that have low betas and
a mix of investments that together create an overall low beta for
your entire portfolio. This will make sure that you survive bet-

ter than those who maybe have a higher rate of return, but if you are withdrawing, the low beta will save your financial life.

> **The Good: Buying mutual funds with low beta if you are retired.**

The Fund's Investment Philosophy

Of course, I look at a fund's investment philosophy, so I can match a fund's philosophy with the needs of my clients. That's obvious. What may not be so obvious is the need to see how well a fund follows the philosophy it puts forth in its own prospectus. This may sound counterintuitive. Can mutual funds really state their investment philosophy in their prospectus and then go ahead and do something else? Yes. In fact, not following the investment path they said they would is one of the biggest complaints the SEC has against funds. Some funds are so egregious at this practice that they have an investment philosophy that's part of a fund's name, such as "growth" or "domestic," but follow another investment strategy than indicted by the name.

A recent study by two universities found that as many as 50 percent of mutual fund managers do things that are either illegal or unethical, or both. That includes things such as buying investments not authorized in the prospectuses, in hope of pumping up returns and attracting attention inside their asset class. The idea is to get a bunch of money in and disguise what they are doing. In cases like this, mutual fund managers take more risk than they are supposed to be taking as outlined in their prospectus.

Disciplined fund companies do not have a problem with this. Those who are not disciplined, often do. When a fund doesn't follow its stated investment strategy, it means when you buy into that fund, you're not getting what you expect and what you have been promised. This makes it difficult, if not impossible, to create a Bulletproofed portfolio because you're not sure what's in your portfolio. Funds that tend to run with the market and ignore their stated philosophy also tend to be higher-risk investments than disciplined funds that stick to their knitting.

PORTFOLIO PUMPING

This is when large mutual funds load up on stocks that make up some of their larger positions. Why buy more of stocks you already have? Because doing so can drive up the price of the stocks. This in turn drives up the value of the fund (because it owns a lot of the stocks being run up). Some funds like to do this at the end of a quarter to make their performance look better. Keep away from such funds.

PORTFOLIO OVERLAP

Portfolio overlap happens when two or more funds in a fund family have many of the same stocks. Some overlap is nearly unavoidable. But some fund companies have lots of the same stocks in a wide variety of funds. The problem with this is that it makes it very difficult for you to diversify. You think you're diversified because you own stock in several funds, only to find that those funds have more similarities than differences. Avoid such fund families.

ANNUITIES

AVOID THE UGLY AND FIND THE GOOD

If you want to make sure your assets are there for your family when you die . . .

If you are concerned about being retired and outliving your money . . .

If you want to make sure your spouse has enough money to live on if something happens to you . . .

If you want a guarantee, no matter what happens in the market . . .

You need to read this chapter.

WHAT ARE ANNUITIES?

Annuities are investments you buy through insurance companies. That's because only insurance companies can create annuities. An annuity is a contract between you (the annuity owner) and the insurance company. You give the insurance company money and, in return, it invests it and guarantees a return of your original principal and sometimes even more than your principal.

There are two basic types of annuities: fixed annuities and variable annuities. The type of guarantee you get depends on the type of annuity you buy. Fixed annuities provide a guarantee that at least your principal and some interest will be returned. Variable annuities, which are like buying mutual funds through an insurance company, guarantee at least your original principal will be returned to your heirs upon your death, which is called the "death benefit." Meanwhile, the value of your variable annuity fluctuates with the value of the mutual fund-like investments (officially referred to as sub-accounts) inside the annuity.

These variable sub-accounts are virtually identical to regular mutual funds you can buy outside of an annuity and are managed by the same big investment company names you already are familiar with. Many variable annuities also offer additional guarantees such as return of principal while you are alive, called "living benefits," and a return of more than your original principal if you die, called "enhanced death benefits," but, of course, for an additional cost. There are no free lunches in the insurance business and actuaries see to that. It's been my experience that most people do not need most of these additional guarantees. They're usually not worth the extra cost.

Let me state here that I don't like fixed annuities and this includes the newest breed of fixed annuities, indexed annuities. A fixed annuity is, in effect, a loan you make to an insurance company. In return, the insurance company guarantees the return of your principal, but generally does not guarantee the exact amount of interest you'll receive. Sometimes there's a guaranteed return, but it's usually an introductory or "teaser" rate for just a limited period, such as one year. Generally, the insurance companies pay you what they feel like paying you. There is usually some kind of very small minimum interest rate guarantee, but it is nothing you would want to earn over the long-term. Historically, insurance companies have tended to struggle financially at times. Their guarantee isn't worth much in a financial downturn because if the insurance company fails they may not be able to repay. Since I'm an advocate of long-term investing, I want the assurance that my money will be protected for years and years, and I don't get this with a fixed annuity. With a variable annuity, on the other hand, annuitants' money is kept in separate accounts and will be there if the insurance company fails.

The Good: Variable annuities have a protection that is not available for fixed annuities. Fixed annuities are loans to the insurance company and if the company goes under, your investments are in trouble. Variable annuity investments are kept in separate accounts and are not subject to the creditors of the insurance companies. If the insurance company goes belly up your investments are still there. This is one of the many reasons I like variable annuities more than fixed annuities.

Also, with a fixed annuity, the insurance company mixes your money into its own general accounts. Fixed annuities can't be used to Bulletproof your portfolio because the insurance company chooses the investments, not you. Historically, fixed annuities have averaged very low returns, many years returning less than the annual inflation rate. Inflation can turn your fixed annuity into a near-worthless piece of paper by the time you withdraw your money.

Enough said. My advice: Don't buy fixed annuities. From here on, we'll focus only on variable annuities.

Variable annuities generally have two phases. The "accumulation" phase, when your contributions (premiums) are allocated among variable sub-accounts and earnings accumulate; and the "distribution" phase when you withdraw money, typically as a lump sum, series of lump sums or through various annuity payment options.

If the payments start immediately, you have an immediate annuity. When you buy an immediate annuity, the insurance company will immediately start sending you money. If the payments are delayed to the future, you have what is called a deferred annuity. You have the insurance company defer distributions until you want to receive them. If you are 55 years old today and plan to retire at age 65, you can buy a deferred annuity with a penalty period that is about seven years, so by the end of 10 years you have complete flexibility of how to take the money out; you can take interest only, take a lump sum, transfer it to another annuity or you can take the very rare approach of annuitizing, which takes out principle and interest.

ANNUITIZATION

Most people think of annuities as financial instruments that provide a guaranteed stream of income to a person for life or a specified period of time. This can be true, but only if you annuitize. The reality is that usually the best use of an annuity is as a guaranteed investment vehicle from which you or your heirs will eventually pull all of the money out without ever annuitizing.

The annuity is not a stream of income until you die. If finances are tight, annuitization can be a smart way to increase your cash flow without the risk of running out of money. Though there are many options for annuitization, the basic idea is that you have an income stream that you can never outlive. Most people don't annuitize, but take money out as they need it. This is good: it helps your principal accumulate. The less you draw out, the more money there is in the annuity to accumulate and grow.

Note: I rarely, if ever, use annuitization. I generally think it is a bad idea for most people. There are some specific circumstances under which it *might* be a viable option, but generally it is rarely needed and not necessary. If you do a good job of planning your assets in the first place, you will not need annuitization.

If you are in a situation that you must use annuitization, you should use variable annuitization. The amount that you receive each year depends on how the investments inside the annuity did that year. If your investments go up 10 percent, your distribution also goes up 10 percent for that year. The opposite is true as well. If your investments drop 10 percent, your distributions also drop 10 percent. Over the long term, if you are in good, solid investments they are going to increase dramatically as ours did during the seven-year period from the beginning of 2000 to the beginning of 2007. If you had been using variable annuitization, your distributions would have almost doubled during that time period. This is the smart way to go for someone who knows that even a small amount of inflation can eat up their income over time unless their investments grow. If the income from your investments isn't enough, this is an option that may work well for you.

SOME BACKGROUND

According to Finetre Corporation, the first fixed annuities in modern times were offered to companies as a way to fund pension plans. These were group annuities, but by the early 1960s individual annuities began to outpace sales of group annuities. The market for annuities in general expanded in the 1970s and 1980s, and the market for variable annuities began its great growth curve in the late 1980s. This can be seen in the growth of investments in variable annuities versus fixed annuities between 1991 and 1994. As of 2000, sales of variable annuities totaled $137 billion, more than twice that of fixed annuities' $53 billion. That's a good thing in my book, because, as I've said before, I typically don't like fixed annuities. (They're usually the bad and the really stupid all in one.)

Finetre attributes the growth in annuities to such factors as:

- A general increase in prosperity for Americans over the long term, which has resulted in more funds available for investment.

- The increase in job mobility in recent years, with the result that the number of employees staying at one company for their entire career has decreased. Partly as a result of this trend, there has been an increased reliance on individual saving for retirement rather than pensions and other employer-provided retirement programs.

CONTRIBUTION AND WITHDRAWAL OPTIONS

There is considerable flexibility in how you buy annuities and how you get your money out. You can buy an annuity by making monthly payments or by investing a lump sum and then making additional contributions whenever you choose. It's just like buying any mutual fund. To take the money out of the annuity you also have many choices. Most annuities give you the option of only withdrawing what you need when you need it, or you can annuitize. Most annuities carry an early withdrawal penalty for some amount of time; if you want to withdraw a lump sum you should know what the penalty is or you may get hit hard.

> **The Good: Flexibility.** One of the strengths of annuities is that they offer a very flexible, extensive menu of payout options. Chances are there's a payout option that will fit the needs of almost every investor.

Here are some of the basic withdrawal options available:

- Partial withdrawal: The most commonly used option is to take out only the amount you need from your annuity when you need it. This can be done upon request or set up to be a systematic distribution from your annuity to meet your current income needs.

- Lump sum: This option pays you all of the funds due to you at one time, in a lump sum.

- Life annuitization: The annuity will continue to make payments for as long as you (or whoever is the annuitant) live. With such an annuity, you do not have to worry about outliving the stream of income provided by the annuity.

- Joint and survivor annuitization: In this case, the annuity continues to make payments for the life of the annuitant and a survivor, who is listed as a beneficiary, such as a spouse. With such an annuity, you do not have to worry about either you or your spouse outliving the stream of income provided by the annuity.

- Period certain annuitization: These types of annuities make regular payments for a specified period time; they continue for that entire period, even if the annuitant dies before the period is over.

These are some of the basic options but the choices can get quite complex. Your financial planner can explain all the nuances and choices available with annuities.

As with mutual funds, you can transfer your money among the sub-accounts available in your particular variable annuity. This is usually free and done without tax penalty. Some annuity companies limit the number of free transfers per year to a set amount, such as 12. As a long-term investor, you are very unlikely to want to transfer more than 12 times a year—and probably won't transfer anywhere near that much.

WHY BUY VARIABLE ANNUITIES?

There are two primary indicators that someone is a good candidate for variable annuities:

1. When I interview prospective clients for the first time, I listen very carefully to what they say. And if I hear a particular word—*guarantee*—I know that an annuity is likely to be in their financial future. If you want guarantees during your retirement—guaranteed income until you die, guarantees your money will be there for your heirs—then you will probably want annuities for part of your investment portfolio.

2. Another tell-tale sign that a prospective client is a good candidate for an annuity is when one partner in the couple (usually the man because 75 percent of the time the woman outlives the man) makes it clear he wants a "good return" and that if something happens to him, his wife will be financially taken care of. He wants to be sure the money is there for her when he dies.

Most variable annuities offer an annual step-up in the amount of the death benefit. That is, each year on your anniversary date, which is the date you purchased the annuity, the death benefit increases to the maximum value your annuity ever reaches on an anniversary date. For example, let's say you bought your annuity for $100,000 on June 1. On the next June 1, it was up to $200,000 but then had dropped to $90,000 on the next June 1 right before you died. Your family would get $200,000 because that was the most your annuity was worth on its anniversary date previous to your death.

With a variable annuity, your return is dependent on the rate of return of the called sub-accounts in the annuity. In theory (though not likely in actuality), these assets could dissipate if the underlying assets disappeared. Variable annuities guarantee that, on your death, your beneficiary will get back at least the money you invested. In some cases, variable annuities offer living guarantees in which, if you keep the annuity for a set number of years, you get your money back while you are still alive—even if the investments go down.

Guarantees are of all different natures, so be careful and understand them fully before you jump. Many of them are a waste of money. The protection here is to work with people and firms of integrity to insure that you get sound advice on whether you need any of these living benefits.

The Really Stupid: Every rider, every additional guarantee, every feature you add to an annuity costs you money—from less than 1 percent to as much as 3 percent, depending on how many and which riders you buy. If your investment advisor wants you to buy all kinds of additional riders, especially ones you do not want or need, watch out. The insurance companies make big money with these riders; the investor often does not.

When I first became a financial planner, and for many years after, I advised my clients that they should first put their money into tax-deductible and tax-deferred investments, then when these were maxed out, into tax-deferred investments and when those were maxed out, into taxable ones. This gave annuities a high priority among the investments I placed my clients in because they are tax-deferred investments. Today, this is no longer the case.

But our government changes its mind periodically, and in the past few years, one change was to lower the capital gains tax rate to a fairly reasonable 15 percent. This has caused me to change my strategy, and I no longer emphasize tax-deferred investments like I used to. If the government changes the tax rate back again, I'll return to my original strategy.

Note, tax-deferred investments have their place, but investments subject to the long-term taxable rate of capital gains can be a better deal than tax-sheltered ones. That's because with tax-sheltered investments, such as annuities, when the money is finally withdrawn it is subject to the ordinary income tax rate, which can run as high as 35 percent. Which is a better deal— 15 percent to Uncle Sam or 35 percent? There are times when you'll want to use tax-deferred investments, but generally, with today's tax rate on long-term investments, I focus on investment vehicles subject to the capital gains rate.

Because of these tax-law changes, I recommend that if you buy annuities, you do so within a tax-deferred and tax-deductible vehicle, such as an IRA. This way you get the benefits that come with annuities, such as a guaranteed return of principal, and there is no tax disadvantage because your IRA is taxed as ordinary income anyway. Again, if the tax situation changes, where the capital gains rate gets close to the income tax rate, then it again will become worthwhile to use annuities for their tax deferral benefits.

Yet, you'll still do well to know about and understand annuities. While not as desirable as they once were in terms of their tax benefits, they are more desirable than ever as a vehicle to provide guarantees.

Then:

The Good: Used to be tax-deductible and tax-deferred investments first.

The Bad: Giving top priority to taxable investments.

Now:

The Good: Still tax-deductible, tax-deferred.

The Bad: Giving just tax-deferred investments top-dog treatment.

The Really Stupid: Not paying attention to changing tax laws.

Of course, there are always exceptions to rules, including some of my rules. I generally do not recommend using annuities in non-IRA accounts, but there can be exceptions where you may want to use an annuity. For example, if you have many other investments, your tax bracket is low or you want the life guarantee. In these cases, you may use an annuity that's not in an IRA or other kind of qualified plan.

The Bad: Proceeds of most variable annuities do not receive a so-called step-up in cost basis when the owner dies. The stepped-up cost basis is the readjusted value of an asset that has appreciated (gone up in value) for tax purposes upon inheritance. With a step-up in cost basis, the IRS says the value of the asset is the market value at the time the asset is inherited, not the value at which it was originally purchased. Other investments, including stocks, bonds and mutual funds, may provide a step-up in tax basis upon the owner's death, but with ever-changing tax laws, these step-up changes may be lost sometime in the future.

VARIABLE ANNUITIES VS. MUTUAL FUNDS

A variable annuity allows you to choose among various investments, such as government bonds, U.S. stocks, foreign stocks and gold. Like a mutual fund, your return is not guaranteed. How well your annuity does financially depends on how well your investments perform. You can, in theory, lose some or all of your money. But if you buy good annuities (such as those I recommend), the likelihood of your getting wiped out is practically nil. Virtually every good mutual fund family like American Funds and Franklin Templeton have their mutual funds available through an annuity.

The Good: Mutual fund returns with guarantees.

From a practical point of view, there are four features of variable annuities not commonly found in mutual funds:

1. Tax-deferred treatment of earnings
2. A death benefit
3. Payout options that can provide guaranteed income for life
4. The living-benefit guarantee—getting your money back while you are still living. If you have a life guarantee in your annuity, you can be guaranteed that if you live, say, 10 years, you can get your money back. This varies based on the annuity contract and every company does its life guarantee in a different way; some are as short as seven years and some are much longer. If you want to make absolutely certain your money will be there for you, that's a good way to do it.

As the Financial Industry Regulatory Authority (FINRA) notes: "A variable annuity's rate of return is not stable, but varies with the stock, bond and money market sub-accounts that you choose as investment options. There is no guarantee that you will earn any return on your investment, but the return of the principle is almost always guaranteed by the insurance company. Due to this risk, variable annuities are securities registered with the Securities and Exchange Commission (SEC). The SEC and FINRA also regulate sales of variable insurance products."

This statement makes variable annuities sound risky. They can be, to an extent, but if you choose your annuities and their investments carefully, there's no reason why they should be risky. As long as you pick great sub-accounts that put their money in investments you are comfortable with, the risk level of a variable annuity will match your personality. Annuities have a number of benefits, including the opportunity for you to make good money safely while Bulletproofing your portfolio, enjoy the power of compounding that comes from tax deferral and, of course, benefit from their guarantees. These are all reasons why they are so useful to retirees.

Benefits of Variable Annuities over Mutual Funds

Variable annuities sometimes provide better performance than mutual funds. How can this be, considering that many annuities are offered by the same companies that offer mutual funds? And, in fact, many annuity sub-accounts are managed by the same teams of analysts and managers as mutual funds. Not only that, but annuities have higher costs than mutual funds, which should put further pressure on the performance of annuities versus mutual funds. There are a few very good reasons why annuities may outperform mutual funds.

1. Buy high, sell low: In volatile markets (and during most of the time in the past quarter century, the stock market has been fairly volatile), people run scared and pull their money out of mutual funds when the market is down, and rush to go into mutual funds when the market is heading up. To cash these people out, mutual fund managers have to keep relatively large amounts of cash on hand (rather than investing it in stocks and bonds) and have to sell when the market is down (that's when people leave) and buy when the market is up (that's when people buy into mutual funds).

This frequent buying and selling takes its toll on the costs of running a mutual fund, on opportunities missed (the hoarding of cash instead of investing) and poor timing of investing (buying when the market is going up and selling when it is skidding lower). These pressures generally are not placed on annuities. That's because the costs of getting out of annuities are so high. Annuities are never to be used as short-term investments, and are not designed to be so.

The discouragements annuities provide investors if they want to cash out means those investors tend to stay in annuities for the long term. It's estimated that about 85 percent of the people who invest in annuities never take the money out. Managers of annuities therefore have a much easier time than their mutual fund counterparts in investing more of their money in stocks and bonds, and don't have to worry nearly as much about inflows and outflows of money, depending on which way the market is heading. The life of an annuity manager is less volatile than that of the mutual fund manager and that works to your advantage.

Keep in mind that the managers of a company's annuity sub-accounts are usually the same as the managers for a company's mutual funds as well. They have the same management objectives, also, and have many of the same stocks. They don't have exactly the same stocks because the stocks are usually bought at different times and in different amounts.

2. Annuities, as strong of an investment choice as they are, are neither as popular or well known nor as appreciated a financial product as mutual funds. As a result, they tend to be smaller; when you have a mutual fund and a "clone" annuity sub-account offered by the same company (meaning that the two financial instruments have the same investment strategy and goals—such as small cap or growth—and often very similar portfolios of stocks), the annuity typically has less money under management than the mutual fund.

Being smaller, the annuity sub-account manager can react quicker to market changes. Also, being smaller, the annuity can invest in smaller, more promising companies. The larger the fund, the larger the companies it invests in. A fund—whether a mutual fund or annuity sub-account—with hundreds of millions or billions of dollars to invest, can't invest in small companies because it means either owning too much of the company (they have a limit of 5 percent ownership in any given company), or having small stakes in too many companies (it would take dozens or hundreds of different small companies to absorb a billion or two of investment dollars from a large mutual fund or annuity).

3. Annuities have contingent deferred sales charges, also known as the penalties for early withdrawals. These force people to stay in the annuity when they might otherwise leave. This, in turn, forces the investor to take a longer-term view of their investments, which is good because there is a 100 percent correlation between the number of trades and a lower rate of return.

> The Really Stupid: The more you trade, the less you make. It's that simple.

> The Good: Like an IRA account, the distribution from an annuity inherited by the next generation can be spread out over the beneficiary's entire lifetime. This decreases the tax hit in any given year and could be a good way to make sure the kids don't blow it all. This can be done through the annuity contract itself; you don't need a will or a trust to accomplish this. Annuities bypass estates, which makes it very simple when settling an estate.

BULLETPROOFING

Both mutual funds and variable annuities provide wonderful Bulletproofing opportunities. Because you can choose from a wide variety of investments, it is possible to use variable annuities to protect against severe recession or depression and runaway inflation, just as with mutual funds. There are mutual fund companies that offer annuities that invest in precious metals securities, foreign government and corporate securities, utility stocks, as well as zero coupon bonds (strips). Nearly complete Bulletproofing is possible with such a diverse portfolio of assets.

ANNUITIES AND RETIREMENT

Retirees don't usually think in terms of aggressive invest-ments. They want conservative investments by the time they are in their 60s, 70s and beyond. But people are living longer than ever. If you retire at 65, you may very well live another 20 or 25 years or more. That's a long time to try to live on just con-servative investments. *Because of their guarantees, annuities are good in-vestment vehicles as a place for retirees to place their more-aggressive investments.* Since the underlying investments are mutual funds, over time the payments to an investor can increase.

Annuitizing today is not what it used to be. It used to be a stream of income as long as you were alive or as long and you and your spouse were alive, and then it was all gone. In today's world, the best annuities are a better proposition. Any annuity principle you haven't used up in your monthly payments goes to your family.

THE DOWNSIDES TO ANNUITIES

Some wrinkles exist with annuities that are not found with a mutual fund. An annuity not held in a qualified plan (IRA, 401K, etc.) functions somewhat like a nondeductible IRA, the kind where you are not eligible to deduct contributions from your taxable income. It, too, has such features as tax deferral and early withdrawal penalties. Yet, one important advantage of an annuity over a nondeductible IRA is that there's no maxi-mum contribution limit to an annuity, unlike the IRA, which has a yearly limit set by the IRS (these limits change over time).

If you withdraw money from your annuity prior to age 59½, the IRS will impose a 10 percent penalty on any money withdrawn that is the result of growth or income (no penalty for withdrawal of principal). There are some exceptions to this, such as the death or disability of the annuitant, where the penalty is not imposed. Because of this potential disadvantage, annuities are generally not appropriate for young people unless part of a retirement plan, such as an IRA, Keogh or pension. Consider using an annuity if you are near or over 59½.

Just like an IRA account, you can withdraw from an annuity before age 59½ if the withdrawals are based on the IRS life expectancy tables. You will not be penalized for those withdrawals but you must continue them until you reach 59½ or for five years, whichever is longer.

> **The Bad: 10% tax-penalty on withdrawals from annuities before age 59½.**

> **The Good: Just like everything in the investment world, if you know how the game is played with annuities, you can accomplish almost anything.**

Early withdrawal charges are among the biggest downside to annuities. Note: Mutual funds do not charge a fee if you withdraw your money early because there are no guarantees associated with them, nor any timetables. The exception to this is B-share mutual funds that have a penalty just like annuities.

The early withdrawal fee with variable annuities is often 5 to 7 percent of the accrued value of the annuity if you take out your money in the first year after purchasing the annuity. The good news is, generally this figure drops each year until the seventh year, after which there are no withdrawal fees. Even during the penalty period, you can almost always withdraw 10 percent to 15 percent without a penalty. You may, however, still incur a tax penalty if you are less than 59½.

Because of IRS and sponsoring company penalties, use annuities only for the long term—more than seven years. The appropriate use of variable annuities is for retirement planning or sheltering income on investments. There is rarely an appropriate use of fixed annuities. I've seen some fixed annuities (remember: these are both bad and very stupid) with withdrawal penalties stretching as long as 20 years. You can't get out of them and they force you to annuitize (at a lower rate of return than you can get elsewhere).

There almost always will be mortality and expense-risk charges imposed by the insurance company for the insurance to cover such items as guaranteed death benefits, annuity payout options that provide guaranteed income for life or guaranteed caps on administrative charges. There are, of course, administrative fees to cover the costs of record-keeping and other administrative expenses. There might be expenses imposed relating to costs involving the investment sub-accounts. And there can be charges for special features, such as a stepped-up death benefit, guaranteed minimum income benefit, long-term health insurance or protection of the value of your principal. The good annuities generally have expenses of 1.50 percent or less. Watch out for the really expensive ones because they are often the worst annuities with the worst investments in them.

To summarize, variable annuities generally have higher fees than mutual funds; fees run about .95 percent to 3 percent annually. There's a reason variable annuities have higher fees than mutual funds—they provide more. They give you guarantees (such as return of your principal, a guaranteed stream of income, et al.) and a life insurance component. Mutual funds don't provide guarantees or insurance. In general, 85 percent of the people who buy annuities don't spend the money from the annuities on themselves, but let it accumulate and pass it on to their children.

It's like cable television—pay only for what you use. You will pay for every variable annuity benefit that comes with your annuity. Spend smart and don't accept any benefits you do not want or will not use.

THE INSURANCE COMPANY

I'm a cautious investor, and like quality in my investments. That's why I study closely not just the annuities I recommend to my clients, but the insurance companies who are offering (and therefore backing) these annuities.

Keep in mind that I generally have my clients buy annuities from two or three different insurance companies. I do that to spread the risk—the risk that an insurance company will go belly up. I believe that it's better to be safe than sorry and since you are counting on your insurance company to pay you for a period of 10, 20, 30 or more years—until you (and maybe your spouse) dies, it's good to spread the risk. An insurance company that's financially solid today might be wobbly a decade or two from now, and it's impossible to know for sure today which insurance companies will be on solid financial ground decades in the future.

My approach has worked well for my clients; their portfolios consistently outperform the market, even during down periods. For example, in the down years following the burst of the Internet bubble in 2000, when most other investors were losing money, my clients' medium-risk portfolios on a year-end to year-end basis were never under water.

CHOOSING AN ANNUITY

Before I discuss how to choose an annuity, let me discuss for a moment how to buy an annuity.

I'm sure there are very competent, honest life insurance agents—people whose sole livelihood comes from selling insurance. I don't know if I've ever met any, but I'll concede there are probably a few out there. But don't bet that if you find someone whose livelihood is entirely dependent on selling insurance, he or she will be competent and honest.

The Really Stupid: Buying an annuity from an insurance agent who sells only insurance.

If you hook up with an insurance agent (who also has a securities license), the chances are good he or she will push annuities on you. (Those who have only a life insurance license can sell only fixed annuities (not variable), but they still push whole or universal life policies.) Why? Because annuities are created by insurance companies and are therefore financial products insurance agents can sell. And sell them they do—however inappropriate an annuity might be for their clients. You are much better off with the advice of someone who can sell you a variety of financial products, such as qualified financial planners. They can pick and choose from what's available to precisely match your needs. If bonds or mutual funds rather than annuities for example, are better for you, your needs, your risk tolerance, then they can sell you bonds or mutual funds.

The Really Stupid: Do not buy investment products from life insurance agents. Never.

Now, back to choosing an annuity. Choosing an annuity is much like picking a mutual fund. You want to study the management, its investment philosophy, and the track record of the sub-accounts. You will also want to carefully consider its cost structure and any restrictions it places on you (such as with-drawal fees). The easier way is to look at the track record of the annuity's comparable mutual fund. Yes, just as with hit movies, annuities sport clones. Many mutual fund firms have their reg-ular funds and then funds in annuities. These mutual fund firms work with insurance companies, which is how they are able to offer annuities, all of which have an insurance compo-nent. The investment philosophies and objectives of the annu-ity sub-account can be identical to that of the mutual fund, though the investments of each may vary.

Why not just look at the track record of the annuity? Because not that many variable annuities have been around long enough to have long-term track records. But if you can find annuities with a track record of at least 10 years, by all means look at their track records rather than that of the related mutual funds.

To find out which "mother" a specific annuity has sprung from, just ask. The mutual fund firm will tell you the annuity's mutual fund proxy. If the mutual fund firm's annuities have sufficiently long enough track records to be meaningful, then just ask for the track record of its annuities, rather than its mu-tual funds. And (to add another plug) by all means contact me to learn of my latest annuity recommendations.

WHEN YOU HAVE A BAD ANNUITY

You may already be an owner of an annuity, but what you own may not be what you should own. You may be in a fixed or indexed annuity. That is bad. You may be in a variable annuity, but it is under performing when compared to the top variable annuities.

You need to deal with such a situation as soon as possible. Usually, the best strategy is to pay any penalties there might be for early withdrawal, and get out. You can oftentimes make back the entire penalty in a single year or a few months if you have really good investments, versus really bad ones. The key is that if you have bad investments, get rid of them and that includes variable and fixed annuities.

How to tell if an annuity is bad:

1. Fixed annuities. Fixed annuities are bad. Do not use them. How do you know if you have a fixed annuity? If you don't have a choice of investments and what you have is an annuity, then it is probably a fixed annuity.

2. Indexed annuities. These are supposed to get the rate of return of the index and have a guaranteed minimum return. What they really do is give you almost nothing above the guarantee. Sometimes the guarantee is questionable because you don't get the entire guarantee as a result of certain conditions they have. They may take away your dividends, which can be important because dividends can be a substantial portion of the total earnings of the index. They often limit the amount of gain you can have in any given year. With all the hooks they put into indexed annuities, they are truly a rip-off.

The Really Stupid: Fixed and Indexed Annuities.

3. Bad variable annuities. Generally speaking, if a variable annuity doesn't have the annuity sub-accounts I recommend available, you don't want it. There are many very expensive variable annuities that provide very little for

the cost. You have to be very careful when buying variable annuities, just as you do with any investment product. Call and get a free copy of my Bruce's Best Annuities list to be sure you are buying the best variable annuities.

Why bother with annuities? For one thing, as I mentioned before, people are living longer than ever. They live longer because of advances in medicine, but these advances usually cost a lot and so medical costs are going up and increasing at a rate faster than inflation. That is a real challenge for retirees. As a result, retirees are at greater risk than ever of outliving their savings. *But by far the most important reasons to buy annuities are the guarantees they provide.* If you want guarantees, annuities are for you. If guarantees are not that important, you likely will want mutual funds. Period.

A RECAP

- Annuities are used primarily for retirement planning and should be considered only as long-term investments.
- Use *only* variable annuities; their payouts vary with how well the annuity sub-accounts perform.
- Do not use fixed annuities. Do not use indexed annuities.
- Buy only those options you really want and need.
- Annuities usually should be inside IRA accounts to avoid any tax disadvantage.
- And remember . . . the only application where I like annuities is where the person wants the guarantees annuities offer and uses annuities only for their riskier investments.

Retirement Planning

The Keys to Financial Security

If you want to make the smart decisions about your retirement . . .

If you want to make sure that you don't outlive the money that you have . . .

If you want to invest the smartest way for retirement . . .

You need to read this chapter.

Virtually all of my clients are retired or are preparing for retirement. Of all the financial concerns facing them, the one they most ask about, the one that concerns them more than any other is that their money will run out and they won't have enough to retire on. Or, as they usually say, "I want to make sure my money does not run out before I die."

Basketball teams usually use one of two philosophies. They have freewheeling offenses, hoping to outscore the other team, or they have detailed defensive plans to limit the other team's ability to score. The freewheelers do okay against weaker teams, but from my observation, they crash and burn when confronted by a well-executed defense. True, the better teams can all shoot the ball, but more importantly, they can play defense. It's usually defense that wins basketball games, and it's defense that wins the retirement game, too. Hoping you will score big between now and retirement to build a tidy nest egg rarely works. Better that you plan defensively now, protect what you have so you are sure you have enough money when the time comes.

How does one accomplish this? It is really quite simple. All you have to do is follow two simple laws: Bruce's first law is 'Don't lose the money' and Bruce's second law is 'See law number 1 and then make a buck.' In other words, Bulletproofing, as discussed in Chapter 1, is the answer.

Many of those who have retired have learned the hard way. Despite a lifetime of work, they don't have enough to make ends meet in retirement or they may have money, but not enough to live the lifestyle they had hoped for. Some must rely on children and other relatives. Others must live in smaller homes or in less desirable locales or just not take the cruises and trips and eat in the restaurants they thought they'd be able to afford.

The challenge many face is that they don't know precisely how much to save. Without clear, specific goals of how much to save, many of us end up putting too little aside. It's much easier to find the determination to save when your goal is specific and you know how much to save and the precise benefits you'll receive.

Our approach to retirement planning is simple to understand and easy to put into practice. You need two skills to create a workable retirement nest egg—planning and determination. Without planning, you can't shrewdly invest your retirement nest egg. Without determination, you'll never save regularly, which means you're unlikely to save enough, ever.

To focus your planning efforts, ask yourself:

- How much income will I need in today's dollars?
- How much income will I have?
- Will my income last?
- What can I start doing now to make sure I have enough later?

Of course, retirement income comes from a variety of sources. Usually, Social Security, pensions and investments provide the bulk of retirees' earnings, although wages and inheritances can be important.

Will my income last? This is an important question, *never* overlooked by those who are retired or thinking of retiring. Keep in mind that people are living longer and will need more money than ever. This, again, means that some of your investments will need to grow over time. It's not enough to have a nest egg sufficiently large enough to cover your expenses on retirement day. You need enough—or earn enough during your retirement—to increase your income sufficiently to not just provide you with a set amount of money each year for as long as you live, but to increase that amount to offset inflation. If you retire at age 65 and inflation averages 5 percent a year, by the time you reach age 75, every $1,000 in income you receive will have a buying power of $614 compared to the day you retired. Put another way, you will need $1,629 when you are 75 years of age to buy what $1,000 bought when you were 65. By the time you reach age 85, $1,000 is buying only $377 worth of goods and services that it bought when you retired. You now need $2,653 to buy what $1,000 bought when you retired.

Let's say inflation runs a more moderate 3 percent a year. After 10 years of retirement, $1,000 will buy only $744 worth of goods and services. You will need $1,344 to buy what cost $1,000 on the day you retired. After 20 years and 3 percent inflation a year, $1,000 buys only $554. You will need $1,806 at age 85 to buy what you were able to buy with $1,000 at age 65. And if you are fortunate to live to age 95, so you are retired for 30 years, you will need $2,427 at age 85 to buy what you were able to buy with $1,000 at age 65. Put another way, $1,000 today buys $412 in 30 years, assuming 3 percent inflation.

Let's look a little closer. Assuming a very moderate 3 percent inflation rate, you will need $1.34 at age 75 to buy what cost you $1.00 at age 65. And by the time you reach 85, you will need $1.81 to buy what cost $1.00 when you were 65. By the time you reach 85, you will need almost twice the income you had at age 65 to live the way you did at age 65. And if inflation averages 5 percent (and it was higher than this in the 1970s, 1980s and into the 1990s), by the time you reach age 79, you will need $2.00 for every dollar you needed at age 65.

I'm stressing the effects of inflation on the buying power of your income because: 1) Inflation is so devastating to one's buying power over time and, 2) Many folks don't appreciate the significance inflation will have on their lives when they retire. If you want your income to keep up with inflation, unless you've got a lot more money than you absolutely need, you will need some of your investments to grow over time. Otherwise, you will be living on income that will buy less and less and your lifestyle and even quality of life will have to decline more and more. And since Americans are living longer than ever, the average person will live in retirement longer than those of any other generation and need to have his or her money last a long time.

I've had a lot of people come into my office and say to me, "Well, we want our last check we write to bounce." But, the reality is, they don't really mean that. To do that, of course is to use variable annuities where you annuitize over the joint life expectancy of husband and wife and the investments are worth zero when they die. They get maximum cash flow while they are alive and leave nothing behind. Cash flow is maximized because the money received is a distribution of both principle and interest.

However, the key for most people is to make sure they protect their principle and that they get a reasonable rate of return.

Seventy percent of my clients use what is called the medium-risk portfolio when they are retired. Its objective is to earn a 12 percent return, and we say if it earns 10 percent, be happy. You don't have to be tremendously aggressive to achieve those kinds of returns, but you need to be willing to take on a risk level in the neighborhood of 50 percent of the market's fluctuations. In our Bulletproof portfolio, we have far exceeded this objective many times. So it is possible to get that return, and even more sometimes, by using Bulletproofing combined with finding inexpensive investments to plug into the asset categories.

Let's now put together a retirement plan for you.

GOAL: HOW MUCH WILL I NEED?

To get an idea of how much you'll need when you retire, think of your needs now. How much would you need if you retired today?

Needs change over time, so you'll have to make accommodations. If you have children, they'll eventually go off on their own (really!). The expense of feeding and clothing them will disappear. Your house may be paid for. Some personal expenses, such as clothing, will probably decline once you are no longer working. There will be grandchildren to shower with gifts. Vacations and travel become more frequent.

The inflation rate for retired people can be much more than the inflation rate you hear about in the news. For example, medical costs are increasing at about twice the rate as inflation. The cause, of course, is because retired people have many more medical problems. After all, as we grow older, we tend to get sick more often.

And a very big change, of course, won't be on the expense side of the ledger, but the income side. You will no longer be working. If you do work, it will probably be a part-time job that pays less or, in some cases, you may be a consultant that actually gets paid more. Sooner or later, almost everyone in retirement wishes to taper down even on the part-time or consulting work and income declines accordingly.

Picture yourself in retirement. Ask yourself these questions:

- How much will you travel?
- How many grandchildren are you likely to have?
- Will you work part-time during retirement?
- Will you keep your home? Will you sell it and rent? Will you owe anything on it by retirement? Will you never own your own home and always rent?

- Where do you want to live? How does its costs compare with your current hometown?

- What situations could force you to take money out of your nest egg before retirement (paying for a child's education, buying a second home, starting a business)?

- Will you want to pursue costly hobbies? How will you fill your time once you stop working?

- Will you take college courses? Courses are now widely available for the retired, some of which require travel. The tuition may be modest, but the cost of travel and accommodations can make them pricey.

Take your current income, add the expenses likely to increase (medical care, travel), deduct those likely to decrease (housing, childcare) and you have an idea, in today's dollars, how much money you'll need when you retire.

Quick Calculation: If you want a quick way to come up with a rough estimate of how much money you'll need in retirement, here's a quick calculation: at a minimum, you'll likely need 100 percent (or close to) the amount you now earn for the first several years of your retirement, and 75 percent of the pretax income you now earn in your later years of retirement.

If you now have a pretax income of $100,000 a year, you will need about $100,000 in pretax income in today's dollars when you retire and $75,000 later on. If you earn $250,000 a year, you'll need $250,000 in pretax income in today's dollars when you retire and $187,500 later on.

The three basic periods of when you retire: At the beginning of retirement, often times people want to spend as much or even a little more then they have been spending because they have a lot of things that they have put off that they would like to do, such as travel. This period tends to be a little expensive.

Then they go into a period where they have got that out of their system. They stay home and want to play with the grandkids. At this time, things are pretty low key and expenses are very low.

The final phase of retirement is when you get ill and die. This tends to be a very expensive time as well. As you can see, there really are three very distinct time periods in retirement and you have to realize that. So if you are spending a little more than you count on in the beginning, that's quite all right. It's normal because after awhile it will probably come way down. And when it's way down, you need to save that money so you can plan for when you get ill.

How do you know how much money you'll need saved up when you retire to produce the income you need? Here's another quick calculation. First, though, do not count your primary residence as part of your assets. Sorry, but, as I've said before, I don't give it any value. That's because you have to live somewhere. If you sold it, you'd have to buy or rent another place. If you own a primary home and a second home you use for vacations or as a get-away, then the second home certainly counts toward your assets if you intend to sell it. You absolutely need one home, but you don't need two.

Now, understanding we don't count your primary residence, add up all your assets. Then, add up the income you expect while in retirement (Social Security, pensions, etc). Let's assume you now earn $150,000 a year and you want $135,000 (90 percent) a year in today's dollars. Let's say you will get $15,000 a year from Social Security and you'll have a pension of $45,000 a year, both of which will increase with inflation. This means you will have an income of $60,000 a year you can count on. This, of course, leaves you $75,000 short of your goal ($135,000 − $60,000 = $75,000).

We'll assume you'll earn 8 percent a year on your money. That's an assumption, of course, but I've produced this amount—and considerably more—for my clients year after year. I consider 8 percent pretty conservative. We'll assume an inflation rate of 3.5 percent a year. To keep up with inflation, you have to increase your income by 3.5 percent a year. We'll assume Social Security and your pension will do this automatically, but the only way you can boost your income from your assets to match inflation is by boosting the amount of your assets by 3.5 percent. We are assuming, here, you never want to dip into your principle and live only on your income. In this way, you can leave your principle to your children or other heirs.

If you earn 8 percent a year and have to leave 3.5 percent of it invested to keep up with inflation, you can withdraw 4.5 percent a year to live on (8% − 3.5% = 4.5%). You need $75,000 a year to begin with (it will increase 3.5 percent a year). Divide $75,000 by 4.5 percent, which is 0.045, and you find you'll need $1,666,666. If you had about $1.67 million and earned 8 percent on it, let it accumulate at a rate of 8 percent a year and withdrew 4.5 percent, you would get an income of about $75,000 a year that would increase 3.5 percent annually and never run out, no matter how long you lived (assuming, again, that you earned 8 percent and took out 4.5 percent).

With these simple calculations, you now know how much money you'll need to live on during retirement and how much money you'll need to save so you can have that amount of income throughout your retirement. Just take the difference in the rate you expect to earn (8% in our example) less how much you have to leave so your assets grow with inflation (3.5% in our example), and divide this by the amount of money you need ($75,000 a year in our example).

If you would like a really straight forward way to calculate how much retirement income you will need, you can find a calculator on our website at www.lefavi.com. This will help you determine how much monthly income your investments may provide you in your retirement. This calculator takes into account all of the things that have an impact on how much income you will receive off of your investments and puts it into an easy to understand report. (You may also look at in the Appendix C to get a better idea of your income and expenses.)

SOCIAL SECURITY

A few comments about Social Security are in order. At the present, there's a lot of talk in Washington about changing Social Security. I don't know if any changes will be made and, if they are, what form they will take. I'm not about to guess, because I don't know what the people in Washington are thinking, or even if they are thinking.

I work on the assumption that for those who are my clients, and that's generally people 50 or older, chances are Social Security will continue much as it is today. There may be some tweaking, such as increasing the amount of income subject to the Social Security tax (it's now the first $90,000 or so of income you earn each year that is subject to the Social Security tax) or increasing the date at which one is eligible for full Social Security (those born between 1943 and 1954 do not get full benefits until age 66). But I don't expect Social Security to change dramatically over the years. I could be wrong, and you certainly need to monitor what Washington is doing in regard to Social Security, but for our purposes, we'll assume it will remain relatively constant.

My recommendation to you about when to start collecting Social Security: take it as soon as you can. This provides a couple of important benefits. It locks in your benefits as soon as possible, so if changes are made to Social Security later, chances are you will be modestly affected, if at all. I believe that those who have yet to start collecting are more vulnerable to changes in the Social Security law than those already collecting.

Also, the earlier you start collecting Social Security, the earlier you can either use this money, or stash it away and save it for later. If you wait a few years to begin collecting your Social Security, you lose the same amount of years when you are not earning returns on this money. If you wait to receive your Social Security money, you will receive more money a month, but it will take a very long time to make up for those lost years.

The return on Social Security is somewhere in the neighborhood of 3 percent. This means if you can take your Social Security payments out and then invest those in something greater than 3 percent, you are probably going to end up a whole lot better off then waiting until you are 66.

If you don't live a really long time, you are going to be a whole lot better off the sooner you take it because you have that many more years of receiving payments from Social Security. I don't know about you, but I feel very strongly that I would like to get back every cent I can from the government because I've paid way more than my share of taxes. All of us have because the reality is there are a lot of people who don't pay who should, such as criminals, illegal aliens and others. I think that makes it harder for the rest of us. That is why I have always been in favor of a national sales tax because that way everyone pays and we could completely do away with the IRS, which would be a godsend to us by getting it out of our lives. The people who spend the most and pollute the environment the most by buying big cars, expensive boats and whatever, are the people who are going to pay the most taxes, so it's environmentally friendly as well.

Every time I've done calculations for clients, it *always* comes up that taking Social Security as soon as possible is the best course.

RETIREMENT ACCOUNTS

Just a few words about Individual Retirement Accounts, SEP/IRAs, 401(k) and 403(b) plans, and the like. Use them to the max. Don't ignore your retirement accounts. They will add up and help provide for you during retirement. I recommend you put the maximum amount of money you can into these accounts for as long as you can, provided they have solid investments and reasonable expenses.

The money that goes into an IRA usually comes from pre-tax dollars, which is very desirable. And with 401(k)s, the employer often matches some or all of your contribution (usually up to some maximum, based on a percent of your contributions). IRS code section 401(k) provides for the employer to offer the employee investments that are tax-deferred. The employer chooses what mutual funds you can utilize and sometimes, unfortunately, they are not very good. Then the employer offers to match a portion of the investors' investments. For example, if you invest 3 percent of your income, they will match that 3 percent. Anything more than 3 percent that you put in is not matched. You should consider putting in the amount that allows you to get the match. However, that is not always a good idea and we will discuss that shortly.

Employers often offer a Roth 401(k) as well. This allows you to put after-tax dollars into a 401(k) that will grow tax-deferred and when they come out, both the principle and the gains on your 401(k) are tax free. However, you still have to pay taxes on the money when it goes in. You should consider a Roth 401(k) if you are a highly compensated employee that can't put very much away because this allows you to put the same amount away, but it all comes out tax free. This is also a good option for young employees who are likely to be in a higher tax bracket when they retire.

Many companies periodically offer their employees early retirement options. I can't tell you here whether such an option is good or bad because the offers vary so greatly and everyone's

situation is different. But let me say this. If you decide to take
an early retirement option, you may be given a choice of keeping your money in the company's pension plan or taking it out
as a lump sum, which you can then invest elsewhere.

Which should you do—keep it where it is or take it out? My
answer to this is, take the money as a lump-sum payment. I assume you're responsible and won't spend the money frivo-
lously. More to the point, I'm assuming you will invest this
money like all your other assets with the goal of providing yourself with a comfortable and secure retirement. Of course, you'll
have to decide where to invest this money. That's what we've
been talking about throughout this book, such as our discus-
sions about mutual funds and annuities.

RETIRING OR LEAVING A COMPANY? TAKE THE MONEY AND RUN.

- There have been many scandals in regard to pension
  plans and the wise thing is to always have control of your
  own money.

- Not only are the opportunities limited, they aren't what
  you want. In particular, you usually can't Bulletproof
  your portfolio in a pension plan. To protect against severe recession and depression, for instance, you need
  Treasuries. Few, if any pension plans offer these. Inflation protection is difficult, if not impossible, because
  inflation-protection investments, such as real estate and
  hard assets, are also not available. (However, these can
  be bought in your IRA).

- Your investment risk is usually higher in a 401(k) than
  outside one. That's because diversification is more difficult. Limited choices are the problem, making it hard to
  achieve the desired degree of diversification. For exam-

ple, domestic stock funds might be available, but not foreign stock funds.

- Pension plan options are often the choice of the bad and the really stupid. For instance, they may have an annuity that provides X number of dollars per month for the rest of your life with nothing left when you die. You have no estate from your pension to pass on to your children.

- You can get capital gains treatment on company stock if it is in your 401(k) plan. One of the smartest things can be if you need a large sum of money immediately after you retire, you can take that stock out of the 401(k) and pay taxes only on your basis. So, if you paid only $1 a share for it and it is worth $100 dollars a share, you only owe ordinary income taxes on the cost basis of the stock. The rest of the gain you pay taxes on when you sell it at capital gains rates that can be as low as zero. This is a one-time option, so make sure you get sound financial advice if you do this.

- On the death of the pension plan participant, if the benefits are left to the estate or a non-see-through trust or the spouse pre-deceases the participant or dies at the same time with no alternate beneficiary, then the only option left is to distribute a lump sum of money a year after the date of death and pay the taxes on the entire amount. In today's tax world, that means the whole thing may be cut in half instead of it continuing in an IRA account for generations.

- Some people believe that if they leave their money in their 401(k), they will save on expenses that can come from things like IRA accounts. Guess what. Those people are wrong. In many of the 401(k) plans today, the employee is picking up the tab on a lot of the expenses, they just don't see it. This is the bad. In fact, in some plans the annual expenses charged to the employees are

3 percent per year. This is usually hidden somewhere deep inside the plan document and oftentimes there are kickbacks and all sorts of incentives to the plan administrator or benefits for the company to keep your expenses high. Get out while the getting is good.

> **The Good: When you leave a company or retire, get your money out of your 401(k) or 403(b) immediately.**

> **The Really Stupid: Leaving it in the 401(k) because you don't know what to do with it. If this is the case, find a good financial advisor and seek their help to get it into some top-flight investments. (If you want to know what the best investments are, give us a call at 800-422-9997 and we will give you the latest list of Bruce's Best Mutual Funds.)**

RECONSIDER INVESTING IN YOUR COMPANY'S 401(K) IF ANY OF THE FOLLOWING SEEM FAMILIAR:

- **High Fees**—As discussed before, 401Ks can have fees in the 2 percent to 3 percent per year range that are the participant's responsibility. Unfortunately, these fees are not evident because they are generally buried in the voluminous plan document. If your fees are indeed that high, and you invest conservatively, it could eat up half of your total return.

In addition, only 37 percent of the companies that offer 401(k) plans pay for even a portion of the expense of its administration. Most of the time, a share of each participant's return is used to fund the administration of the plan.

- **Conflicts of Interest**—Administrators often make up the cost of supplying the plan to their 401(k) participants by deducting various fees from the employees' accounts, and by charging the mutual funds for "shelf space." Basically, they force various mutual fund companies to pay them to be in their 401(k) plan. This tends to lead to really lousy mutual funds since the good companies don't have to pay to be included and the ethical ones won't.

- **Hidden Fees/Kickbacks**—Some 401(k)s receive payments from mutual fund companies to carry their funds in the plan. These payments do not come out of their pockets, but out of yours. This is done by incorporating hidden fees such as a "sub-transfer agent fee" and/or "12B-1 commission" which are both buried in the individual fund's expenses. By doing this it can end up costing two times as much as if you were to purchase the mutual fund outside of a 401(k).

- **Lousy Mutual Fund Investments**—401(k)s are often stocked full with the worst of the mutual fund world because of the often-included pay-for-plan feature. The plan administrator, or the company, has in the past been paid directly or indirectly for the mutual funds it utilizes. In fact, some companies have in the past created their own mutual funds and actually make money on their 401(k) plans, which most attorneys consider to be illegal. 401(k) plans are supposed to be solely for the benefit of the workers, not the companies.

- **Profit Centers**—A small plan administrator sometimes charges $500 to set up a small plan and $1,500 per year to maintain it. Most employers think this will cover all expenses, but it doesn't always work out that way. Plan administrators will sometimes place participants in very high-cost investments. These higher-cost investments can run more than twice as much as you would have to

pay if they chose a lower-cost mutual fund for that very
same investment.

The answer here is simple: The management of any company should always choose the best mutual funds available, pay
the plan administrator separately (which avoids a conflict of interest) and the fees should be nominal.

AVOIDING THE 10 PERCENT EARLY WITHDRAWAL PENALTY

If you withdraw from your IRA before reaching 59½ years
old, you will be assessed a penalty from the IRS. It is possible to
get around the 10 percent early withdrawal penalty if your money
is in an IRA and you withdraw it for the following purposes:

- For individual health insurance premiums if you are
  unemployed.
- Withdrawal of $10,000 for a first-time homebuyer.
  This is someone who has not owned a home for the
  past two years.
- Paying you or your families cost for higher education.
- You can take out distributions based on your life expectancy
  and pay no penalty, no matter what age you take it out.

Most of these options are available in an IRA, but not in a
401(k). Always roll over your 401(k) when you change companies or retire.

If you have a bad 401(k) with lousy investments and really high
expenses (your employer is required to give you a copy of the plan
document so that you can see what the expenses are) you should
not put any money into the plan. You might consider adding to
the plan, but only to the extent of the matching provided you are
not going to work for the employer for a very long time. Figure 6

Figure 6: Comparison of Contributions into a 401K Plan
or a Taxable Account over 30 Years

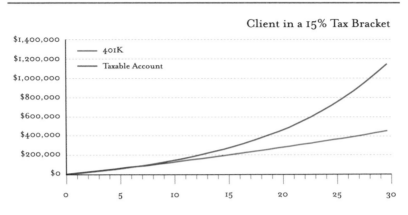

Client in a 15% Tax Bracket

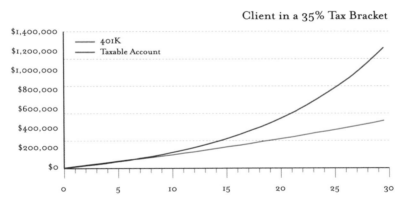

Client in a 35% Tax Bracket

clearly shows that whatever your tax bracket, if you have a lousy 401(k) plan and you are going to be with that employer for seven years or more, you are better off not contributing.

The time period is much shorter if you have the option of putting the money into a Roth IRA as can be seen in Figure 7. If you have a rotten plan and you think you may be at an employer for more than three years, you may want to opt for a Roth IRA instead of putting your money into a terrible 401(k).

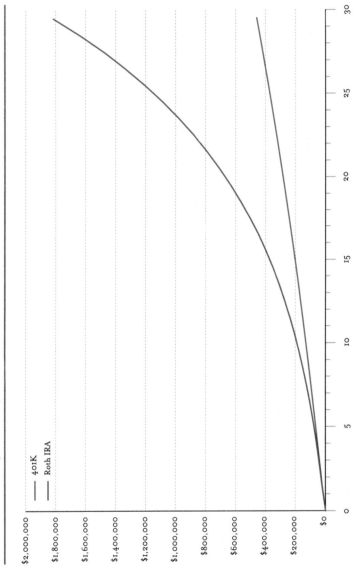

Figure 7: Comparison of Contributions into a 401K or a Roth IRA over 30 Years

Trusts

To Trust or Not to Trust—That Is the Question

If you want to make sure your money isn't chewed up by attorneys or estate taxes . . .

If you want to make sure your nasty cousin doesn't get your kids . . .

If you have a complex estate with a privately held business or land in more than one state . . .

If you want it to be easy for your family to settle your estate . . .

You need to read this chapter.

Estate Planning: It protects you when you are alive and helps your family when you are dead

If you don't have any heirs—children, charitable institutions, relatives, and friends—well, you probably don't need estate planning because you're not too concerned with what happens to your money when you die. If this is the case, you can skip this chapter, unless you are concerned about asset protection. In most cases, when you improve your estate planning, you also improve the protection of your assets while you are alive.

For most people, a trust and a will is a better answer than a will. A trust is the most important estate-planning instrument available. Let me tell you a true story that illustrates this. There was a financial planner who worked for me whose mother was living in Provo, Utah. She died with only a house, some personal assets in the home and no investments. As simple as her estate was, he still ended up making six trips to Provo from Salt Lake City (close to an hour's drive each way) and spending as much as half a day in court each time waiting to speak to the judge in order to settle his mother's estate. After that experience, he decided he was going to recommend to all of his clients that they have a trust, simply because of the hassle involved with not having one. If you want to reduce hassle for your family, a trust and a will are a must.

The Really Stupid: Dying intestate.

If you are like most people and have assets you hope to pass on to others, estate planning should be very important to you. If you don't plan well for what happens to your estate when you die, then your state government, via the probate court, will do it for you, and there's no telling what will happen with any assets that remain at the time of your death. Government has enough trouble taking care of itself. I, for one, wouldn't want it in charge of my finances when I die. One of Bruce's Laws is 'No matter how bad something is, the government will make it worse if it gets involved.' Without a will or instructions for passing on your estate to your heirs, you die intestate, which means you leave the government, lawyers and others to deal with your estate. With proper, effective estate planning now, you can minimize the involvement of the government and others with your estate when you die.

The Bad: Dodging discussing the topic of your own death.

Let's face it; dealing with one's death is not a happy topic. Death is a topic many prefer to avoid considering. For others, they procrastinate about their estate planning because they feel their death and that of their spouse is far off and there's no rush to engage in estate planning. This helps explain why so many avoid drawing up wills, trusts and other plans for what happens to their property once they are dead. Because any of us can suddenly come down with a fatal illness or suffer a fatal accident, such procrastination is a major mistake.

The Good: Now is the time to put your estate planning in order. It doesn't matter how old you are, how many heirs you have or how much money is likely to be in your estate when you die, there's no better time than now to complete your estate planning. Good estate planning helps protect your assets while you are alive and helps make things easier on your family when you die.

And More Good: In addition, discuss your estate plans with your children and other heirs. Don't be secretive about what assets you have, where they are and what plans you are making for these assets. Many difficulties and tensions that come after a person's death come from the surprises to heirs about the plans they didn't know anything about.

Studies have shown that in states where they have ways of keeping track of funds under the purview of estate planning attorneys, these types of attorneys were responsible for more thefts from clients than all other types of attorneys combined. By having your heirs be part of your planning process, conflict between your heirs is less likely. This means that it is less likely estate attorneys will get involved with your estate. This has the wonderful advantages of lowering attorneys' fees and lessening the chances of an attorney making off with your money. The bottom line: The people you want to get your money are more likely to actually do so.

We'll discuss here the basics of estate planning. Keep in mind that estate planning can be very complex, as it deals with legal and tax issues that are often open to interpretation. Plus, heirs have been known to get into big, brawling fights over estate plans. For these reasons, I very strongly encourage you to see an estate planning expert.

Use only the very best estate planning attorneys because the standard wills and trusts will not get it done.

This is not an area of your financial plan that you should do yourself or leave to someone you know who seems "knowledgeable" about estate planning. Everyone's estate plans are different, and I can't explain here all there is to know. I can, however, give you some pointers that will help you work with a professional.

WILLS

A will is a legal document that explains in detail where you want the assets of your estate allocated after debts and taxes are paid. Without a will, state law will dictate what happens to your estate's property. In addition to specifying what happens to your assets, a will names who will oversee the execution of the will. This person is called the executor or personal representative. It can also name who will care for your children if you die while they are still minors.

You may think your will covers everything, but unless you are very careful, you can miss important details. The results of such mistakes can be disastrous for your heirs and for any plans you had. For example, you may specify in your will that your spouse gets your entire estate. That seems clear. But is it? If an ex-spouse is still listed as the primary beneficiary of your life insurance policy and retirement account, he or she will likely get those assets and not your current spouse. If an ex-spouse is listed as the primary beneficiary on any other type of account that bypasses probate, such as annuities, then the ex-spouse could end up with many of the assets in your estate instead of your current spouse.

Let me also briefly discuss the executor of your estate. This person will be overseeing the financial matters concerning your estate. It helps if you choose someone with some financial savvy who wants to see your financial desires carried out. Definitely, choose an executor who is organized and good with details, because keeping track of everything—the sale of assets, the location of assets, the disbursement of assets, the payment of taxes, the necessary communications with heirs, etc.—is difficult at best. You will probably need someone with political skills, especially if conflicts among the heirs are likely. The executor, ideally, should be able to disperse tensions and emotions and be a calming influence as well as a leader. Consider writing a letter of instruction. Though not a legal document, it expresses what you want, such as the location of important documents and assets, and funeral arrangements.

I've drawn up a simple form to track important documents called the Lefavi Locator and I urge you to use it. Not too long ago, I had a gentleman call me and ask if I was the Bruce that used to work at Westinghouse in Los Angeles. It turned out he was an engineer that I had worked with for years. He had heard my show on how using a Lefavi Locator was so important because it clearly lays out where all your important documents are, which can save your family tremendous time and headaches at your death. He had done something similar to that in organizing his father in-law's estate and every time he and his wife's family get together, they all thank him for making it so easy to settle his estate. He came in and got five copies of a Lefavi Locator so that everyone in his family could fill out one in case something happened to them.

I have helped settle estates many times and some of them turn into Easter egg hunts where we are looking for all of the assets. In some cases, it takes years to find all of them. It turns out to be tremendously expensive due to the legal fees and very stressful for the family. This is one of the most important but simple steps you can take to make settling your estate easy. If you make filling out the Lefavi Locator found in Appendix D the first step in planning for death, it will make the process much easier for everyone involved.

TRUSTS

A trust is a legal agreement set up under state law that you, as grantor, establish to facilitate the transfer of property to a manager, called a trustee, for the benefit of your heirs (beneficiaries). The assets you put in the trust are owned by the trust and no longer owned by you.

Trusts allow probate avoidance because the assets of a trust are no longer owned by the person, they are owned by the trust. When the person dies, the probate court is only interested in the person's assets and since the trust's assets are now owned by the trust, not the person, those assets bypass probate.

An advantage of this is lower taxes. Some—but not all— trusts provide tax benefits. For example, a bypass trust (also called a credit shelter trust) can eliminate or reduce federal estate taxes. This is a standard part of an inter vivo or living trust. Married couples use it when their estate exceeds the amount exempt from federal estate tax, which we'll assume is $2 million per person. A married person may leave an unlimited amount of assets to his or her spouse, free of estate taxes and without using up any of the estate tax credit. The problem is that if the second or surviving spouse then dies with an estate worth more than the exempted amount ($2 million), his or her estate is subject to estate tax. Meanwhile, the first spouse's estate tax credit was unused and, in effect, wasted because they did not use a trust.

> The Good: Living trusts or revocable trusts are difficult, if not impossible, to overturn if there is a dispute. There might even be tough provisions where, if a person disputes the trust, he or she is cut out of the trust completely.

The bypass trust, upon the death of the first spouse, establishes a separate, irrevocable "bypass" trust with the deceased spouse's share of the trust's assets. The surviving spouse is the life beneficiary of this trust, with the children as beneficiaries of the remaining interest. Normally, the life beneficiary has the income from the trust plus 5 percent of the principle per year. The irrevocable trust is funded to the extent of the first spouse's exemption. Thus, the amount in the irrevocable trust is not subject to estate taxes on the death of the first spouse, and the trust takes full advantage of the first spouse's estate tax credit. This type of trust can be complex (which is true of virtually all issues relating to trusts) but a bypass trust helps larger estates pass on assets to children while minimizing taxes. Note: a bypass trust, also called a marital trust, is revocable until death, then, upon death, the bypass trust becomes irrevocable. A lot of attorneys use two trusts from the very beginning: a "his" and a "her" trust, and then on the death of one spouse, that spouse's trust becomes irrevocable. This helps with the asset protection issues earlier referred to.

A trust is also a good way to control how your property is distributed. The grantors can use a trust to maintain control by drawing up the trust documents or giving directions to the trustee on how they want the assets used and the trustee then needs to follow those directions.

The most important thing that a trust does for you is that it reduces the hassle for your family and the cost of settling your estate. The minute you die, the surviving trustee can take over by giving someone you have an account with a copy of the trust and your death certificate. This is very quick, very inexpensive and doesn't require any court appearances.

There are many types of trusts. Here are some of the more common ones:

Revocable Trust

Revocable trusts let you retain full authority of the assets you put in your trust. You or any other person or organization can be the trustee. They are used to manage your assets and avoid probate. They generally do not provide any tax advantages. However, a living trust can give you an estate tax advantage.

In order to set up a trust, you must have a signed document that has the following things in it:

1. You must name someone as the trustee who can mange the assets that you have in your trust. You can name yourself or your wife as the trustees initially.

2. You must name a successor trustee. This is a person who will manage your trust after you, your wife or both of you die. This person will distribute the assets to the beneficiaries.

3. This document must specify what investments, assets and properties you put into the trust.

4. The trust must name beneficiaries. That is, the people that are going to receive the assets of the trust. Initially, if you are married it may be your spouse and then the children after that. This is a very important part of the trust.

5. The fact that you can change or revoke your trust at any time.

6. Special provisions you might have due to your individual situation.

HOW A REVOCABLE LIVING TRUST FOR A FAMILY WITH CHILDREN AS BENEFICIARIES WORKS

1. Husband and wife transfer shared property to trust. (Each spouse can also transfer individually owned property.)

2. Husband dies. Trust property is divided in half.

3. Wife can use income from husband's trust and up to 5 percent of the principle each year, as she chooses. She has the ability to spend anything in her own trust. Upon her death, the principle of the husband's

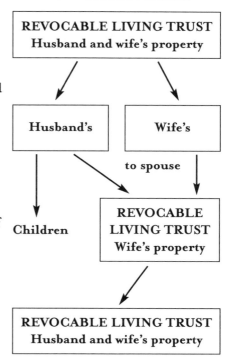

trust goes to the children as well as the principle from her trust.

4. Wife's property stays in living trust until spent or her death.

Irrevocable trust

With this type of trust, you enter into a permanent arrangement that can't be revoked or changed. You have control in the sense that you set up the trust in the way you want, but once set up, you give up control. In return, there can be tax advantages because the assets in the trust may no longer be considered part of your estate for tax purposes. The trustee can be given discretionary powers and with some qualifications, beneficiaries may have a say as to what happens to the assets in the trust. But, as the donor, you normally must be out of the picture for the trust to be effective as a tax-saving device. An irrevocable trust is a separate tax entity that pays tax on its accumulated income. An irrevocable trust typically can be used to provide gifts to beneficiaries without incurring a gift tax.

The Really Good: Living Trust (*inter vivo*)

Living Trusts

Living trusts are set up while you're alive. You can be the trustee, though you usually will name someone to take over when you die or are incapacitated. This type is used as a tool for asset management and as a way to transfer property without having to go through the probate process. These generally do not provide any income tax advantages, but can allow you to transfer twice as much on an estate tax basis to the next generation without taxation.

Charitable Remainder Trust

Gifts to charitable organizations can provide you with tax write-offs today, even if the organization doesn't receive the gift until many years from now, through the use of a charitable remainder trust. With these trusts, you receive the income from the trust as long as you and your spouse are alive. Upon the death of the two of you, what remains in the trust goes to charity. The good thing is, you get a tax deduction now for that future gift. Sales of any highly appreciated property you have inside the trust are not taxed once you place it in a trust. This can be a big advantage in creating a higher income for you while you are alive and provides a nice charitable gift upon your death.

The Really Stupid: Testamentary Trust

Testamentary Trust

This type of trust is created by the terms of your will (testament) after you die and is funded by your estate. You name the trustee in your will. This is used to save on estate taxes and having someone you want manage the assets in the trust. Note, with a testamentary trust, your estate still ends up going though probate and you still have the expense of setting up a trust. The attorney gets you twice: once for setting up the trust and then for probating the estate on top of that. The double-shaft, I call it.

WILLS VERSUS TRUSTS

Should you have a will instead of a trust?

Yes, if all of the following statements apply to you:

- Your estate situation basically is uncomplicated (that is, you have no investment real estate, no family owned businesses, etc.).
- Your will is not likely to be contested or disputed by any of its potential heirs.
- Your estate is not large. That is, it does not contain a great sum of money or unusually valuable items (that go beyond such things as your house, home furnishings, etc.). More than $2 million in total assets is a good rule of thumb to measure the definition of large.
- Your assets are held mostly in joint tenancy. Rights of survivorship are clearly assigned. This will ensure your assets are transferred directly to the surviving tenant with no interference by the probate court.
- You have any disputed property. The court during the probate process can often better settle this circumstance. Probate removes all claims, thereby unequivocally settling any and all previous disputes.
- You are young, healthy and unlikely to die for a long time. Preservation of assets is not the principle concern because you haven't accumulated much yet.
- Insurance to protect the spouse and children in case it is needed, bypasses probate. By using payable-on-death accounts and tenancy with rights of survivorship you can bypass most of the need for probate and have a very simple situation. Payable-on-death accounts can be set up with most bank accounts or stock brokerage firm accounts.
- You have creditors and complicated debt problems. Probate provides an absolute cutoff time notification

for creditors to file claims. A trust does not create any such cutoff period. Problems like these can be run through probate and the rest of the assets put in the trust and hopefully bypass the probate process.

Or, should you have a will and trust?

Yes, if any of the following statements apply to you:

- Your estate is likely to be disputed. If there is any worry of this happening, a trust should be used, as it is a much more powerful document than a will and very difficult to break.

- Your estate is rather complex. The more complex your estate, the greater the probate costs will be in processing a will. Using a trust dramatically reduces those potential costs.

- You want to avoid the typical delays associated with probating a will. The greater your assets, the greater the potential delays. Delays, in turn, increase the probate costs of a will. Many probate cases have remained in court for more than 10 years, costing millions of dollars.

- The possibility exists that you or your spouse may not be competent at some time to manage your estate's assets. If this is the case, a trust is a wise idea, since you can appoint a trustee today to manage the assets in the future.

- Your estate is worth more than a single person can transfer to the next generation, so you need a trust to cut down your estate taxes.

- You have a privately held business. If you have such a business, when your will is probated or if you die intestate, the probate process is public information. That could be very detrimental to your business or your heirs.

- You or your spouse has been divorced. (Again, your ex-spouse can end up with your money if you really screw up.)

- You have investment real estate holdings in more than one state. In this case, the attorney in your home state talks with the attorney where your other real estate is located, and they burn up your estate. It is almost guaranteed that the estate planning attorneys are going to rip you off.

- You have significant assets beyond your retirement needs and the assets have to go some place.

- If disability is something you are concerned about, whether you are disabled now and fear it will become worse or that you will become disabled soon and won't be able to manage your own assets, then a good living trust is imperative.

- If the state you are in establishes a set percentage of your assets as a fee to the attorney, you must have a trust to avoid those outrageous fees.

- If privacy is of great of concern. There is virtually no disclosure with a living trust and if you have a privately held business, privacy should be of concern because your competitors can find out all about your situation through probate.

An attorney told me a story about a client of his who had only a will and was the owner of a construction business. Upon his death, the business became part of the probate process. As the probate progressed, the wife found she desperately needed some additional funds to take care of some emergency expenses. A competitor found out through probate about this need because she only had a will and therefore her information was not private. He called her and negotiated a ridiculously low price on some equipment she had that the competitor wanted for his business. This is one reason it is critical that if you are a small business owner you retain privacy by using a will with a living trust.

Here are some tips for establishing your trust:

- Fund your trust. The trust works *only* if your assets are in the *name* of the trust. Otherwise, those assets are forced to go through the probate process. You will have wasted all the money you spent to create your trust, but worse, you will have failed to evade the "demon probate" and its enormous costs, taxes, and delays.

- Do not use "testamentary" trusts. Some states do not recognize these as valid trusts, which may complicate your IRA accounts. (The same applies to wills containing "pour over" provisions.) The testamentary trust may be forced into the probate process, causing funds to be spent to create a valid trust. Hence, the testamentary trust was unable to protect the money and failed all together to prevent probate. There are so many potential pitfalls with testamentary trusts that I advocate never using them.

Taking Advantage of Unlimited Exclusions for Estate Tax

- Another's tuition. You may pay another individual's school tuition, but that is all. Books, supplies, dormitory rent, board and room, and similar costs are *not* permissible. You may, however, make a $12,000 gift to that individual in addition to his tuition, as there is an unlimited exclusion for tuition. The tuition payment must be made by you—*not* by the student—directly to the institution.

- Another's medical expenses. An unlimited exclusion exists also when you want to pay another person's medical expenses. It applies in the same manner as for tuition. Again, be certain that *you* pay all money and pay it directly to the medical provider.

Preventing Undesirable Situations

- You determine the time your beneficiaries inherit. Although the law states when an individual "legally" becomes an adult, you are the better judge of the maturity of those who will inherit your assets. Using a trust enables you to set the time or age when an individual may receive the assets.

- Again, probate brings on publicity. During probate proceedings, things that you wish to keep private can become public information, even printed in newspapers. A testamentary trust or a will *cannot* prevent this from occurring. All possibilities of publicity can be erased *only* through the use of a living trust. This is another reason we do not recommend a testamentary trusts.

- *You* make the guardianship decisions. A guardian can't be appointed through a trust, so you have to appoint one through your will. Be very precise in your will of whomever you wish to be the legal guardians of any minor children you have. A will is used to designate a guardian for the children of a deceased individual. Without this, your children are at the mercy of the judge and court's decision. Your evil sister-in-law could end up with guardianship of the children if this is not properly spelled out in your will.

- Not your first marriage?—Decide whose children get what. If you have remarried but wish the bulk of your assets to go to your own children, you must make the correct provisions in a trust. Otherwise, the current spouse's children stand to get all . . . and your own children nothing.

- Make time today to set up a proper will or trust. Even the most "adventurous" sort has to face reality: none of us are getting out of here alive. So, you better get prepared! Otherwise, you can expect a court-appointed attorney (picked randomly) to act as the administrator of every little bit of your worldly goods, deciding willy-nilly who gets what. If none of that bothers you, then by all means don't bother with those pesky wills or trusts.

Rest comfortably knowing that a sizable portion of your estate will go to that "administrator" you never laid eyes on, and even more of your money will go here and there for other little court costs. If, however, you would prefer that family, friends, organizations, or charities receive your estate, set up a living trust. You can appoint who you want to be the administrator (family, friend, etc.), and it may cost little or nothing to your estate compared to the court-appointed routine. If you insist on a lot of risk and danger, why not go bungee jumping—but don't confuse risk and danger with foolhardiness. Complete your living trust or will *before* that jump!

- Remember, setting up a trust does not eliminate the need for a will. The will is necessary to catch anything you might forget to put into your trust- items so trivial that you don't want to list them in attachments to your trust.

- A will or a trust does not help you avoid nursing home costs.

- The most important thing that a trust does for you is that it reduces the hassle for your family and reduces the cost of settling your estate. The minute you die, the surviving trustee can take over by giving someone you have an account with a copy of the trust and your death certificate. This is very quick, very inexpensive and doesn't require any court appearances.

When setting up a trust, it is important to do four things:

1. Set up a trust using a skilled attorney.

2. Keep the trust current. Review the trust at least once every five years

3. Put all your assets that can be put in the name of the trust, into the name of the trust. This way, it is operated on by the trust and doesn't have to go through probate. Anything not named in the trust must go through probate unless it, by definition, bypasses your estate such as an IRA account.

4. Use the Lefavi Locator so that your family doesn't have to go on an Easter egg hunt to find all of your important documents.

These are the keys to making things easy for you and your family in organizing and settling your estate.

In Appendix E, you will find a Post-Mortem checklist. If someone in your family dies, this is the checklist that we recommend you use to make sure you haven't forgotten anything. There are quite a few things and some of them are a bit technical. A good financial advisor can help you with these so that you don't have to run up a big bill with an attorney. Always get as much done as you can and get as well organized as you can before you go into see the attorneys to keep the fees to a minimum.

APPENDIX A: DECLINE OF VALUE OF A CERTIFICATE OF DEPOSIT

Year	CD Rate*	Top Federal Tax Rate**	Avg. State Tax Rate***	Inflation Rate****	Real Return
1967	5.19	70.0%	5.0%	3.1	−1.8025
1968	5.97	75.3%	5.0%	4.2	−3.020925
1969	7.34	77.0%	5.0%	5.5	−4.1788
1970	7.64	71.8%	5.0%	5.7	−3.9237
1971	5.21	60.0%	5.0%	4.4	−2.5765
1972	5.01	50.0%	5.0%	3.2	−0.9455
1973	9.05	50.0%	5.0%	6.2	−2.1275
1974	10.02	50.0%	5.0%	11	−6.491
1975	6.9	50.0%	5.0%	9.1	−5.995
1976	5.63	50.0%	5.0%	5.8	−3.2665
1977	5.91	50.0%	5.0%	6.5	−3.8405
1978	8.6	50.0%	5.0%	7.6	−3.73
1979	11.42	50.0%	5.0%	11.3	−6.161
1980	12.94	50.0%	5.0%	13.5	−7.677
1981	15.79	50.0%	5.0%	10.3	−3.1945
1982	12.57	50.0%	5.0%	6.2	−0.5435
1983	9.28	50.0%	5.0%	3.2	0.976
1984	10.71	50.0%	5.0%	4.3	0.5195

Year	CD Rate*	Top Federal Tax Rate**	Avg. State Tax Rate***	Inflation Rate****	Real Return
1985	8.24	50.0%	5.0%	3.6	0.108
1986	6.5	50.0%	5.0%	1.9	1.025
1987	7.01	38.5%	5.0%	3.6	0.36065
1988	7.91	28.0%	5.0%	4.1	1.1997
1989	9.08	28.0%	5.0%	4.8	1.2836
1990	8.17	28.0%	5.0%	5.4	0.0739
1991	5.91	31.0%	5.0%	4.2	−0.4176
1992	3.76	31.0%	5.0%	3	−0.5936
1993	3.28	39.6%	5.0%	3	−1.18288
1994	4.96	39.6%	5.0%	2.6	0.14784
1995	5.98	39.6%	5.0%	2.8	0.51292
1996	5.47	39.6%	5.0%	3	0.03038
1997	5.73	39.6%	5.0%	2.3	0.87442
1998	5.44	39.6%	5.0%	1.6	1.41376
1999	5.46	39.6%	5.0%	2.2	0.82484
2000	6.59	39.6%	5.0%	3.4	0.25086
2001	3.66	39.1%	5.0%	2.8	−0.75406
2002	1.81	38.6%	5.0%	1.6	−0.57916
2003	1.17	35.0%	5.0%	2.3	−1.598
2004	1.74	35.0%	5.0%	2.7	−1.656
2005	3.73	35.0%	5.0%	3.4	−1.162
2006	5.24	35.0%	5.0%	3.2	−0.056

* 6 month CD rate average—per federal reserve   **Average Return   −1.446808875**
** per IRS
***assumed average state tax rate
**** per Bureau of Labor Statistics

APPENDIX B: TYPES OF MUTUAL FUNDS

The Investment Company Institute classifies U.S. mutual funds in 33 investment objective categories. These should be of interest to you, not just to give you an idea of how large a variety of mutual funds exists, but because if you are to properly diversify, you need to buy a basket of mutual funds that invest in a variety of different types of investments. If you own, say, six mutual funds, and five are aggressive growth funds, or three invest just in pharmaceuticals, you are not properly diversified, even though you hold shares in a variety of mutual funds.

Let me make a point here: We occasionally use exchange-traded funds and usually do not recommend any kind of index funds, including exchange-traded funds, except where you might use them at the end of a tax year to take a tax loss on a mutual fund. You have to leave it out of the mutual fund for 30 days, so you put it into an exchange-traded fund of the same type of the mutual fund at no cost even if it's a load mutual fund because, if you keep something out for 90 days in most funds, you can still put it back at no cost. You recognize your loss, have a nice tax advantage and it costs you almost nothing because you use an exchange-traded fund as the parking place while you have it out of your position.

Here are the descriptions of various mutual funds according to the ICI:

Equity Funds

- *Capital Appreciation Funds* seek capital appreciation; dividends are not a primary consideration.
- *Aggressive growth funds* invest primarily in common stocks of small, growth Companies.
- *Growth funds* invest primarily in common stocks of well-established companies.
- *Sector funds* invest primarily in companies in related fields.
- *Total Return Funds* seek a combination of current income and capital appreciation.
- *Growth-and-income funds* invest primarily in common stocks of established Companies with the potential for growth and a consistent record of dividend payments.
- *Income-equity funds* invest primarily in equity securities of companies with a consistent record of dividend payments. They seek income more than capital appreciation.
- *World Equity Funds* invest primarily in stocks of foreign companies.
- *Emerging market funds* invest primarily in companies based in the developing world.
- *Global equity funds* invest primarily in equity securities traded worldwide, including those of U.S. companies.
- *International equity funds* invest primarily in equity securities of companies located outside the United States.
- *Regional equity funds* invest in companies based in a specific part of the world.

Hybrid Funds

- *Hybrid funds* may invest in a mix of equities, fixed-income securities, and derivative instruments.

- *Asset allocation funds* invest in various asset classes including, but not limited to, equities, fixed-income securities and money market instruments. They seek high total return by maintaining precise weightings in asset classes.

- *Global asset allocation funds* invest in a mix of equity and debt securities issued worldwide.

- *Balanced funds* invest in a mix of equity securities and bonds with the three-part objective of conserving principal, providing income, and achieving long-term growth of both principal and income. These funds maintain target percentages in asset classes.

- *Flexible portfolio funds* invest in common stocks, bonds, other debt securities, and money market securities to provide high total return. These funds may invest up to 100 percent in any one type of security and may easily change weightings depending upon market conditions.

- *Income-mixed funds* invest in a variety of income-producing securities, including equities and fixed-income instruments. These funds seek a high level of current income without regard to capital appreciation.

Taxable Bond Funds

- *Corporate Bond Funds* seek current income by investing in high-quality debt securities issued by U.S. corporations.

- *Corporate bond funds—general* invest two-thirds or more of their portfolios in U.S. corporate bonds with no explicit restrictions on average maturity.

- *Corporate bond funds—intermediate-term* invest two-thirds or more of their portfolios in U.S. corporate bonds with an average maturity of five to 10 years. These funds seek a high level of income with less price volatility than longer-term bond funds.

- *Corporate bond funds—short-term* invest two-thirds or more of their portfolios in U.S. corporate bonds with an average maturity of one to five years. These funds seek a high level of income with less price volatility than intermediate-term bond funds.

- *High-Yield Funds* invest two-thirds or more of their portfolios in lower-rated U.S. corporate bonds (Baa or lower by Moody's and BBB or lower by Standard and Poor's rating services).

- *World Bond Funds* invest in debt securities offered by foreign companies and governments. They seek the highest level of current income available worldwide.

- *Global bond funds—general* invest in debt securities worldwide with no stated average maturity or an average maturity of five years or more. These funds may invest up to 25 percent of assets in companies located in the United States.

- *Global bond funds—short-term* invest in debt securities worldwide with an average maturity of one to five years. These funds may invest up to 25 percent of assets in companies located in the United States.

- *Other world bond funds,* such as international bond and emerging market debt funds, invest in foreign government and corporate debt instruments. Two-thirds of an international bond fund's portfolio must be invested outside the United States. Emerging market debt funds invest primarily in debt from underdeveloped regions of the world.

- *Government Bond Funds* invest in U.S. government bonds of varying maturities, seeking high current income.

- *Government bond funds—general* invest two-thirds or more of their portfolios in U.S. government securities of no stated average maturity. Securities utilized by investment managers may change with market conditions.
- *Government bond funds—intermediate-term* invest two-thirds or more of their portfolios in U.S. government securities with an average maturity of five to 10 years. Securities utilized by investment managers may change with market conditions.
- *Government bond funds—short-term* invest two-thirds or more of their portfolios in U.S. government securities with an average maturity of one to five years. Securities utilized by investment managers may change with market conditions.
- *Mortgage-backed funds* invest two-thirds or more of their portfolios in pooled mortgage-backed securities.
- *Strategic Income Funds* invest in a combination of U.S. fixed-income securities to provide a high level of current income.

Tax-Free Municipal Bond Funds

- *State Municipal Bond Funds* invest primarily in municipal bonds issued by a particular state. These funds seek high after-tax income for residents of individual states.
- *State municipal bond funds—general* invest primarily in single-state municipal bonds with an average maturity of greater than five years or no specific stated maturity. The income from these funds is largely exempt from federal as well as state income tax for residents of the state.
- *State municipal bond funds—short-term* invest primarily in single-state municipal bonds with an average maturity of one to five years. The income of these funds is largely exempt from federal as well as state income tax for residents of the state.

- *National Municipal Bond Funds* invest primarily in the bonds of various municipal issuers in the United States. These funds seek high current income free from federal tax.

- *National municipal bond funds—general* invest primarily in municipal bonds with an average maturity of more than five years or no specific stated maturity.

- *National municipal bond funds—short-term* invest primarily in municipal bonds with an average maturity of one to five years.

Money Market Funds

Taxable Money Market Funds invest in short-term, high-grade money market securities and must have average maturities of 90 days or less. In actuality, most money market funds run their funds by using maturities up to one year. These funds seek the highest level of income consistent with preservation of capital (i.e., maintaining a stable share price).

- *Taxable money market funds—government* invest primarily in U.S. Treasury obligations and other financial instruments issued or guaranteed by the U.S. government, its agencies, or its instrumentalities.

- *Taxable money market funds—non-government* invest primarily in a variety of money market instruments, including certificates of deposit from large banks, commercial paper and bankers' acceptances.

- *Tax-Exempt Money Market Funds* invest in short-term municipal securities and must have average maturities of 90 days or less. In actuality, most money market funds run their funds by using maturities up to one year. These funds seek the highest level of income—free from federal and, in some cases, state and local taxes—consistent with preservation of capital.

- *National tax-exempt money market funds* invest in short-term securities of various U.S. municipal issuers.
- *State tax-exempt money market funds* invest primarily in short-term securities of municipal issuers in a single state to achieve the highest level of tax-free income for residents of that state.

Keep in mind that this is just one way of categorizing mutual funds, though ICI is certainly a very respected organization in the investment field. I won't go into too much detail on how others do it, but here's a quick look at how Morningstar [www.morningstar.com], which is a very reputable source of information on mutual funds, breaks down stock mutual funds:

DOMESTIC-STOCK FUNDS

Morningstar defines mutual funds with at least 70 percent of assets in domestic stocks as domestic stock funds. These, in turn, are divided into nine categories:

- Large growth
- Large blend
- Large value
- Medium growth
- Medium blend
- Medium value
- Small growth
- Small blend
- Small value

Morningstar defines "large" as large capitalization companies, namely those that make up the top 72 percent of the domestic U.S. market. Medium companies are the next tier, making up 18 percent of the domestic U.S. market in terms of their capitalization, while the small cap stocks are those making up the smallest 10 percent of the U.S. domestic market.

As of April 2002, companies with market caps of greater than $8.85 billion were deemed to be large; those between $1.56 billion and $8.85 billion were mid-cap, while those smaller than $1.56 billion were small.

Value refers to funds that invest in stocks their managers believe are undervalued. The stocks are worth significantly more than their current price, the fund manager thinks, and therefore they're good values. What constitutes an undervalued stock is, like beauty, in the eyes of the beholder. Definitions can vary from fund to fund. The same is true of growth funds. These funds invest in companies that have better-than-average growth prospects, though how those prospects are calculated varies from fund to fund.

Here is a type of fund that many investors should pay attention to. In addition to funds that use value and growth (or a combination of both) as an investment strategy, Morningstar also looks at domestic-equity funds that specialize in a particular sector of the market. When you invest in such funds, you are diversifying within an industry, but not across industries. The so-called sector funds include:

- Communications
- Financials
- Health care
- Natural resources
- Precious metals
- Real estate
- Technology

- Utilities
- Convertible bond
- Domestic hybrid
- (Precious-metals funds are assigned to the international-stock asset class.)

International-Stock Funds

Stock funds that have invested 40% or more of their equity holdings in foreign stocks (on average over the past three years) are placed in an international-stock category.

Europe: at least 75% of stocks invested in Europe.

Japan: at least 75% of stocks invested in Japan.

Latin America: at least 75% of stocks invested in Latin America.

Diversified Pacific: at least 65% of stocks invested in Pacific countries, with at least an additional 10% of stocks invested in Japan.

Asia/Pacific ex-Japan: at least 75% of stocks invested in Pacific countries, with less than 10% of stocks invested in Japan.

Diversified Emerging Markets: at least 50% of stocks invested in emerging markets.

Foreign: an international fund having no more than 10% of stocks invested in the United States.

World: an international fund having more than 10% of stocks invested in the United States.

International Hybrid: used for funds with stock holdings of greater than 20% but less than 70% of the portfolio where 40% of the stocks and bonds are foreign.

You can see that there are many ways to look at mutual funds. Recognizing the differences is important because you need a variety of funds to be properly diversified and you need to understand the risks involved with investing in any individual fund. With these categories from ICI and Morningstar, you pretty much know all the different types of funds available to you.

APPENDIX C: INCOME AND EXPENSES CALCULATION

	BUDGET	ACTUAL	DIFFERENCE
INCOME			
Wages & Bonuses			
Income from interest			
Income from investments			
Income from Social Security			
Other			
Subtotal			
TAXES WITHHELD			
Federal			
State & Local			
Social Security/Medicare			
Subtotal			
Spendable Income (Income minus taxes)			
EXPENSES			
HOME			
Mortgage/Rent			
Insurance			
Property Taxes			
Repairs/Up-keep/HOA			
Improvements			

	BUDGET	ACTUAL	DIFFERENCE

UTILITIES
Electricity
Water & Sewer
Gas
Telephone—land line
Telephone—cellular

FOOD
Groceries
Eating out
Other (coffee, etc.)

MEDICAL
Insurance
Out-of-pocket medical
Prescriptions/Medication

TRANSPORTATION
Car payments
Gasoline
Repairs/Maintenance
Insurance
Other

**ENTERTAINMENT/
RECREATION**
Cable TV
Movies
Internet
Hobbies
Subscriptions
Vacations

WARDROBE
Clothing
Shoes
Jewelry
Accessories
Dry Cleaning

GROOMING
Hair
Make-up
Gym
Toiletries
Other (massage, nails etc.)

	BUDGET	ACTUAL	DIFFERENCE
PETS			
Food			
Grooming			
Boarding			
Veterinarian			
FAMILY OBLIGATIONS			
Day Care/Babysitting			
Child support			
Alimony			
MISCELLANEOUS			
Cleaning products			
Household products/Décor			
Gifts/Donations			
Other			
INVESTMENTS & SAVINGS			
(how much you contribute)			
401(k)			
IRA			
Stocks/Bonds/Mutual Funds/CDs			
Savings (Cash)			
College Fund			
Emergency Fund			
Other			
TOTAL EXPENSES			
Surplus or Shortage			
(Spendable income minus total expenses)			

Appendix D

Name: _____

LOCATION AND VALUE
OF IMPORTANT DOCUMENTS

CHECK ITEMS THAT ARE APPLICABLE TO YOUR SITUATION AND STATE THE <u>EXACT</u> LOCATION OF EACH AND VALUE WHEN APPLICABLE:

DATE: _____

PERSONAL INFORMATION

☐ Adoption papers _____

☐ Ante nuptial agreement _____

☐ Automobiles: Titles _____

☐ Bank account (Checking) # _____

☐ Bank account (Safe Deposit Box): _____
Key location: _____

☐ Bank account (Saving) # _____

☐ Bills of sale _____

☐ Bills payable: Annually _____

☐ Bills payable: Auto _____

☐ Bills payable: Monthly _____

☐ Bills payable: Quarterly _____

☐ Bills payable: Utilities_____

☐ Birth certificates _____

☐ Cemetery deed _____

☐ Credit cards #'s _____

☐ Credit cards #'s _____

☐ Credit cards #'s _____

☐ Deeds of property _____

☐ Deferred compensation agreement_____

☐ Divorce decree _____

☐ Employee benefit records_____

☐ Family genealogy _____

☐ Income & gift tax returns _____

☐ Insurance auto _____

☐ Agent: _____   Phone#_____

☐ Insurance auto _____

☐ Agent: _____   Phone#_____

☐ Insurance fire-casualty_____

☐ Agent: _____   Phone#_____

☐ Insurance health & accident _____

☐ Agent: _____   Phone#_____

☐ Insurance life (term)_____

☐ Agent: _____   Phone#_____

☐ Insurance life (whole life) _____

☐ Agent: _____   Phone#_____

☐ Leases_____

☐ Marriage certificates _____

☐ Military papers _____

☐ Mortgages & notes owed _____

☐ Mortgages & notes owned _____

☐ Naturalization papers _____

☐ Payroll check stubs _____

☐ Prenuptial agreement _____

☐ Separation agreement _____

☐ Social Security papers _____

☐ Tax returns income & gift _____

☐ Trust documents _____

☐ VA records _____

☐ Wills _____

☐ Other _____

BUSINESS INFORMATION

☐ Business continuation agreement _____

☐ Business entity papers _____

☐ Business legal records _____

☐ Buy/Sell agreement _____

☐ Key man insurance _____

☐ Partnership agreement _____

☐ Tax information _____

☐ Other _____

INVESTMENT INFORMATION

☐ Broker/Dealer (Financial Planner) _____

☐ Phone # _____

☐ Record of investments _____

Approximate value of investments: _____

☐ Annual income _____

☐ Annual income (spouse) _____

☐ Annuities (fixed) _____

☐ Annuities (variable) _____

☐ Annuities (variable) _____

☐ Bonds (note maturity date) _____

☐ CDs _____   Maturity Dates: _____   Held at: _____

☐ CDs _____   Maturity Dates: _____   Held at: _____

☐ Income property _____

☐ Mutual Funds _____

☐ Mutual Funds _____

☐ Retirement plans _____

☐ Stock redemption _____

☐ Stocks (certificate?) _____

☐ Stocks (certificate?) _____

☐ Stocks (certificate?) _____

☐ Stocks (non-certificated) _____

☐ Stockholders' agreement _____

☐ Tax receipts _____

☐ Gold Coins/Collectibles _____

☐ Mechanic's Name _____

APPENDIX E: POST-MORTEM CHECKLIST

At the time of death, the Personal Representative and/or the Successor Trustee is requested to do the following:

1. Contact attorney to assist with the following:
    a. Determine whether a probate is necessary or advisable.
    b. Determine whether there is a need to file estate tax returns, either federal or state. The Federal Estate Tax Return is due nine (9) months from the date of decedent's death.
    c. Assist in transferring assets to the proper beneficiary (i.e., revocable trust, beneficiaries of personal property, etc.).

2. Funeral and burial arrangements.
    a. Verify funeral and burial preferences as set forth in a Letter of Instruction to Personal Representative, if any, or discuss with the family.
    b. Contact funeral home relative to execution of funeral and burial arrangements. You should shop around for prices as they may vary greatly.

    c. Determine decedent's desires relative to anatomical gifts. Specifically, review Uniform Anatomical Gift Act Statement of gift and make proper arrangements, if appropriate, for anatomical gifts.

3. Obtain certified copies of death certificate for use where needed.

4. Winding up decedent's personal affairs.

    a. Arrange to have mail forwarded.

    b. Determine whether credit cards should be canceled.

    c. Determine whether or not utilities should be continued. Check on deposits with utility companies and request a refund, if appropriate.

    d. If the decedent was a tenant, notify the landlord of the date the premises will be vacated and request refund of the security deposit.

    e. Examine policies of insurance (fire, theft, and casualty) on real estate or tangible personal property. Have policies endorsed to the estate and, if necessary, increase the amount of insurance coverage or terminate coverage.

    f. Determine whether or not locks should be changed on decedent's residence.

    g. Terminate any further Social Security checks.

    h. Determine if there is any litigation involving the decedent. Immediately seek legal counsel on what steps should be taken.

5. Identify and locate decedent's assets.

    a. Prepare a detailed inventory of assets of decedent and obtain the fair market value of each asset as of the date of death. Obtain appraisals as needed. Determine title to all assets.

b. Locate and safeguard items such as jewelry, coin and stamp collections, gold and silver collections, artwork, furs, valuable books, checkbooks, bank savings pass books, certificates of deposit, bank statements, stock certificates, bonds, investment records, brokerage house statements, and insurance policies.

c. Take possession of contents of decedent's safety deposit box.

d. Determine and collect any amounts owing to the decedent as of the time of death (income tax refunds, promissory notes, etc.).

e. Apply to Social Security Office, railroad, or other federal programs for any death or survivor benefits. Where appropriate, contact Veterans Administration to obtain veterans benefits.

f. Determine the existence of any life insurance policies and make application and claim for payment of proceeds pursuant to the insurance policies. Determine specifically whether or not accidental death benefits are payable. Check with credit card companies and credit unions to see if there are any insurance benefits relating to those accounts.

g. Determine whether assets to be gifted to charity should be distributed now (i.e., assets that have expenses that exceed income such as non-income producing real estate) or held until the last possible minute in order for the family to continue to earn interest (monetary gifts) on those assets.

6. Decedent's debts and estate administration expenses.

a. Make sure all debts are paid, including attorneys' fees, before making any charitable distributions.

b. Determine if a final income tax return must be filed and file if necessary.

c. Determine if an estate tax return needs to be filed and file if necessary.

d. Determine if a checking account is necessary in order to pay the decedent's debts and estate administration expenses.

e. Determine what expenses, debts, and other obligations of the decedent need to be paid. Specific attention should be addressed to payment of any estate taxes.

7. Distribution of assets.

a. After payment of expenses, obligations, and taxes, make proper distribution of the assets of the decedent's estate.

b. Consider a petition to obtain court approval of distribution or sale of assets.

c. Obtain Receipts and Releases from distributees to establish amount and nature of distributions.

d. Beneficiaries should decide whether or not they will disclaim (refuse) any part of their inheritance. If so, they must do it in writing to the trustee or executor within 9 months of date of death, and they may not use or benefit from the disclaimed property. Disclaimed property will pass through to alternate beneficiary as designated in will or trust.

8. Valuation Date.

a. It will be important to decide whether the valuation date is the date of death or six months later, as allowed under the regulations.

b. It will be highly advantageous to choose the correct valuation date.

c. This should be discussed with your financial advisor.

9. IRA Accounts.

a. The following decisions regarding IRA accounts must be made by the indicated date, the year after the date of death; these decisions include the following:

- September 30th—Final determination of beneficiaries. This is where the other September 30th decisions below come from.

- September 30th—For anyone disclaiming their share of the accounts the deadline for making a "qualified disclaimer" is generally nine months after Participant's death

- September 30th—Payout of any amounts due to charities, estates or other undesirables that can adversely affect or take away the stretch out for individuals and avoid any IRA account being declared as having no beneficiary.

- October 31st—If a "Qualified" trust is the primary beneficiary of the IRA account, then provide a full trust document to the IRA custodian along with a letter from the trustees stating that the beneficiaries will not be changed. This can also be done upon account opening as well to avoid missing the above deadline. This establishes the trust as a "Qualified" trust, which means it will not be subject to the 5 year rule. IRA assets can be left in and taken out as RMDs base on the trust beneficiary's life expectancy (or the shortest life expectancy in the case of multiple beneficiaries).

- December 31st—If multiple beneficiaries, split IRA account into the different beneficiary names. This gives each beneficiary maximum benefit, especially on RMDs, Spousal Rollover option (if spouse), and withdrawal options.

b. If the client has sufficient funds already in their estate, should they disclaim IRA or pension plan inheritance, in favor of contingent beneficiaries in order to reduce their estate taxes?

c. If the spouse is not the sole beneficiary, look for ways to remedy the problem, i.e. splitting inherited IRA by 12–31 of year after participant's death.

d. Should the IRA account be left in the name of the participant? Consider this if the spouse is under the age of 59½ and needs to make withdrawals. Also consider leaving part of IRA in participant's IRA, the amount the spouse may need to withdraw penalty free before she turns 59½ and rollover the rest to the spouse's own IRA for better beneficiary treatment.

e. If Participant dies on or after the RMD (required minimum distribution) RBD (required beginning date), then the beneficiary must make sure that the RMD has been or is taken out for the year in which the participant dies at the participant's distribution rate. This **HAS** to be done before year end. For subsequent years, it depends on who the beneficiary is and what they do with the IRA account.

f. Properly title a non-spousal beneficiary IRA.

g. IRA beneficiary should Take IRD deduction if estate taxes are paid by decedent's estate.

h. Do not make changes to IRA if possibility of disclaimer.

i. Check and see if surviving spouse may have a right to statutory share.

APPENDIX F

Important Disclosures

- The Lefavi Medium-Risk Portfolio is a model portfolio comprised of multiple investments allocated to various asset categories based on Modern Portfolio Theory. The goal is to meet or beat the long-term U.S. stock market average with half the risk.

- The Dow Diamonds is an exchange-traded fund that holds the 30 stocks that comprise the Dow Jones Industrial Average.

- The Vanguard 500 is an index fund that seeks to track the performance of the S&P 500 index.

- The NASDAQ Composite Index is an index that comprises a universe of 3,000 stocks that trade on the NASDAQ Stock Exchange. For comparison purposes we used the NASDAQ Composite index because there is no actual investment that has tracked the entire NASDAQ index over this same time.

- Model assumes that changes to allocation percentages were made only once a year on January 1. Actual client portfolios are changed at different times of the year and may be changed more then once in accordance with material economic and market factors. Due to a major mandatory change for all clients on July 1, 2006, the model incorporated this change to the allocation for the remainder of the 2006 calendar year.

- The Lefavi Portfolio assumes the portfolio was held for the entire year and perfect balance was maintained throughout the year.

- The investments used for each asset class in the Lefavi Portfolio were the most commonly used investments in each given year.

- In actual portfolios, other investments may have been used depending on specific portfolio limitations and/or client preferences.

- The model portfolio represents an ideal portfolio and is not typical of all client portfolios.

- Portfolio returns are adjusted to reflect a total client management fee of 1 percent. Because each client's portfolio is charged differently based upon portfolio composition, we determined, on average, our clients pay 1 percent per year in total management expenses. Therefore, the returns stated above are net of all fees.

- Mutual fund and exchange-traded fund returns used for comparison also reflect a 1 percent average management expense just as if clients under our management held them.

- The Lefavi Model Medium-Risk Portfolio is the most commonly used model portfolio with our clients; other models exist that may have had higher or lower returns and risk levels.

- Model assumes reinvestment of all dividends and short- or long-term capital gains.

FIGURE 2:

Client starts out with $500,000 and withdraws $35,000 (7%) at the end of each year for 25 years. Scenario 1 (6 month CD) shows the value of the clients account each year after taxes and inflation if they had been invested in 6 month CDs. Scenario 2 (Inv. Company of America) shows the value of the clients account each year after taxes and inflation if they had been invested in Investment Company of America. The client that has their money in CD's runs out of money in 15 years. The client in ICA never runs out of money, and, in fact, never falls below the initial $500,000 they put in.

FIGURE 3:

This graph compares the growth of $100,000 from 1/1/2000 to 12/31/2006 for an investment in 6 month CDs, the DOW Diamonds ETF, the Vanguard 500 fund, and the Lefavi Medium Risk Portfolio. Returns are net of all expenses but do not reflect tax or inflation rates.

FIGURE 4:

This figure shows what the NASDAQ composite index did from the beginning of 1986 to the end of 2006 based on the year-end closing value of the index.

FIGURE 6:

This figure addresses the question of whether it is more beneficial to contribute to a lousy 401K plan, or to invest the money in a taxable investment account.

The first graph in this figure shows a client in a 15% tax bracket contributing $10,000 per year pre-tax to their 410K with their employer matching $3,000 per year compared to the client paying the taxes on the $10,000 and investing the remaining $8,500 in a taxable investment account. The 401K receives a net return of 2% per year and grows tax deferred, but client pays 15% tax when it is withdrawn while the taxable account returns 8.5% per year after tax (10% minus capital gains rate of 15%).

The second growth shows a client in a 35% tax bracket contributing $10,000 per year pre-tax to their 410K with their employer matching $3,000 per year compared to the client paying the taxes on the $10,000 and investing the remaining $8,500 in a taxable investment account. The 401K receives a net return of 2% per year and grows tax deferred, but client pays 35% tax when it is withdrawn while the taxable account returns 8.5% per year.

FIGURE 7:

This figure addresses whether it is more beneficial to invest money in a 401K or a Roth IRA.

The graph shows a client in a 15% tax bracket. Client is in 35% tax with the client contributing $10,000 per year pre-tax to their 401K with their employer matching $3,000 per year compared to the client investing the $10,000 per year in a Roth IRA. The 401K receives a net return of 2% per year and grows tax deferred, but client pays 15% tax when it is withdrawn while the Roth IRA returns 10% per year.

Lefavi Wealth Management
2323 Foothill Drive, Suite 100
Salt Lake City, UT 84109

(801) 486-9000
(800) 422-9997
www.lefavi.com